Return to the

Water

A Feminine Guide to Self-Exploration, Pleasure, and Expression.

Galilani Ahawi

Honeylee Williams

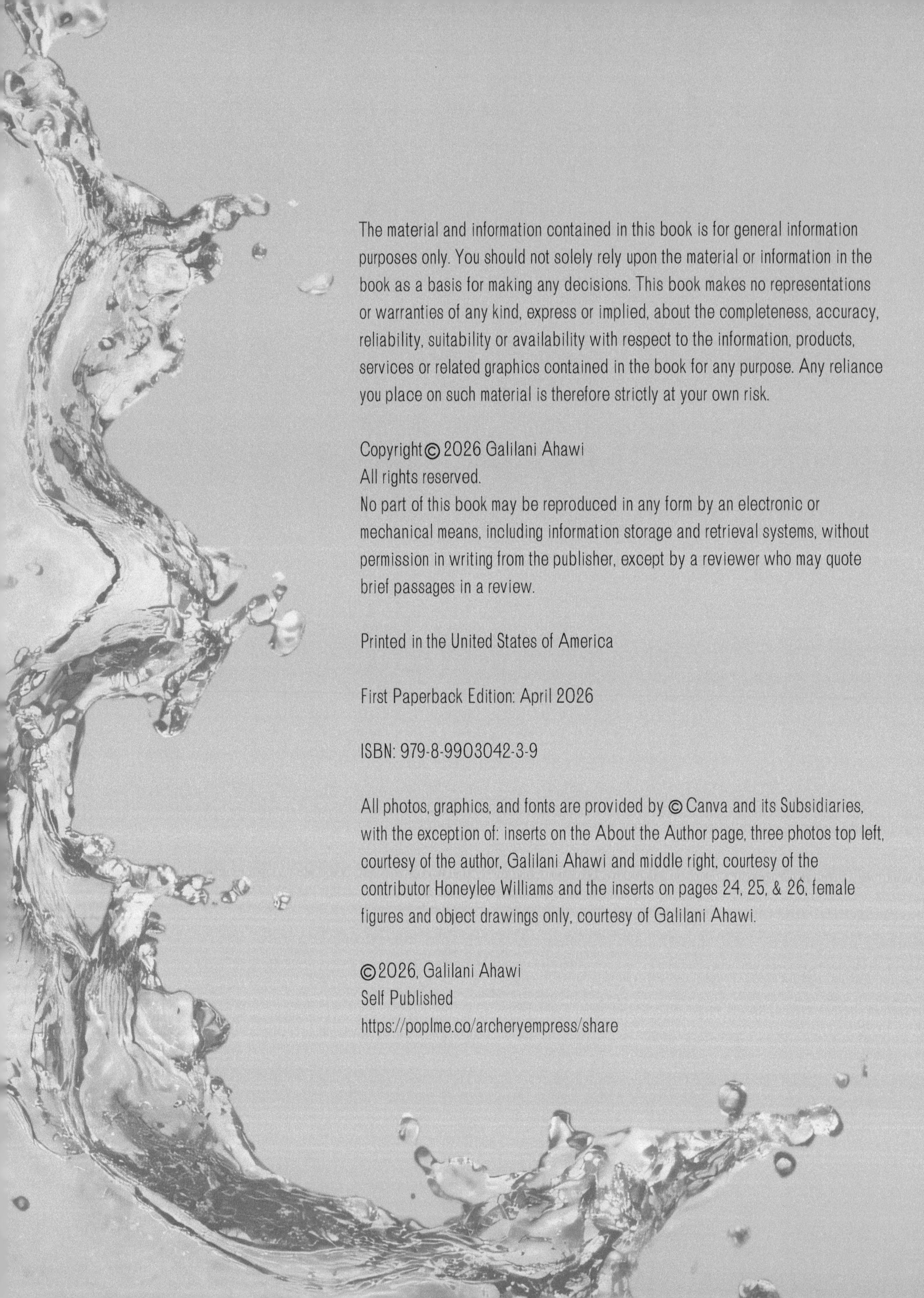

Disclaimer

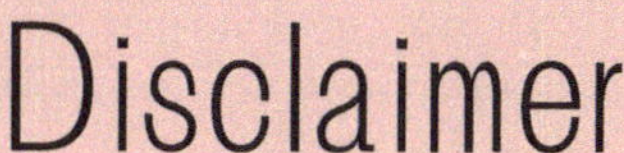

The publisher and author offer this book and its contents on an "as is" basis, without making any representations or warranties regarding the book or its contents. They disclaim all such representations and warranties, including but not limited to warranties of healthcare, skill, and personal safety. Furthermore, they take no responsibility for any errors, inaccuracies, omissions, or inconsistencies found within. The author and publisher do not guarantee the accuracy, completeness, or timeliness of the information provided in this book.

The publisher and the author make no guarantees concerning the level of success you may experience by following the advice and strategies contained in this book, and you accept the risk that results will differ for each individual. The testimonials and examples provided in this book show exceptional results, which may not apply to the average reader, and are not intended to represent or guarantee that you will achieve the same or similar results. It is recommended to seek advice from a legal or qualified professional regarding the suggestions and recommendations in this book. Except where explicitly stated, neither the author nor the publisher, nor any contributors or representatives mentioned in the book, will be held liable for any damages resulting from the use of this book. This limitation of liability covers all types of damages, including compensatory, direct, indirect, consequential damages, loss of life, property damage, or claims from third parties.

The supplements, nutraceuticals, essential oils, fatty acids, probiotics, and other items listed in this work are examples of functional foods and how they can be used to help, support, promote, and maintain different ailments and the symptoms associated with said ailments. The information, including but not limited to, text, graphics, images and other material contained in this book are for informational purposes only and is not intended to diagnose, treat, cure, or prevent any condition or disease. It is important to note that this book is not a substitute for professional advice from a licensed legal, healthcare, or other professional. Always consult with a licensed professional to ensure you are making the best decisions for your specific situation. By using this book, you acknowledge and accept this disclaimer.

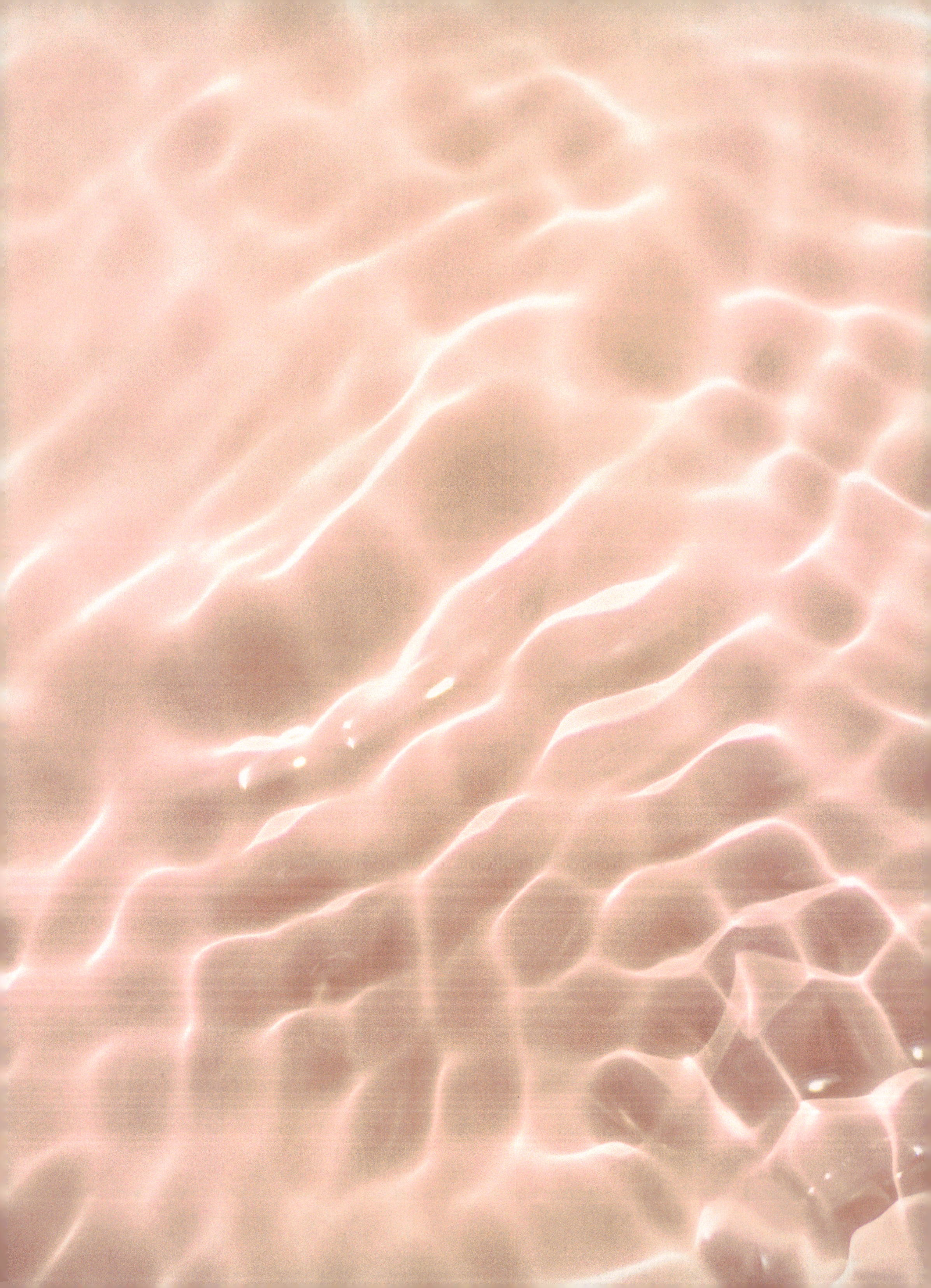

ABOUT THE AUTHOR

GALILANI AHAWI
"ARCHERY EMPRESS"

As a survivalist and unapologetic advocate for women's self-sufficiency, I approach the body the same way I approach the wild: with respect, curiosity, and the belief that every woman deserves the right of knowledge and self-expression. With a blend of science, real-life experience, and refreshing honesty, I present this book to my readers. Whether I'm teaching women how to survive in the wilderness or how to reconnect with their own bodies, my message is clear. I'm not just educating; I'm helping women take their power back.

SPECIAL CONTRIBUTOR

HONEYLEE RAE WILLIAMS

As a newly divorced woman and a proud mother of four, I am stepping into a new chapter of life with strength, resilience, and purpose. After years of putting others first, I am rediscovering myself mentally, physically, and emotionally, and embracing what it truly means to live as a healthy, whole, and independent woman. Part of that journey is reconnecting with my confidence and embracing my sexuality without shame, understanding that it is a powerful and natural part of who I am. Ladies, it is never too late to become the woman you were always meant to be. This is my time to rebuild, to thrive, and to inspire others to do the same.

SCAN FOR MORE INFO

The Dynamic Duo

Honey and I go way back since middle school. I'm 37 now, so you do the math. We've seen each other grow from girls into women, into mothers, into survivors of life in ways only we fully understand. We were even pregnant at the same time with our firstborn daughters, stepping into motherhood side by side like we had done everything else.

For a while, life kept us close, physically and emotionally. We lived near each other, stayed in each other's lives daily. But life has a way of shifting things. She moved away, and somewhere along the journey, we lost touch. Not because the bond wasn't real, but because sometimes life just be lifeing.

Years passed, and somehow, like it was always meant to, we found our way back to each other a few years ago. And when I say we picked right back up and got even closer, I mean that. Now she's in Arizona, and I'm still in Georgia, the same place where our story started.

We've both been through it. She's endured some soul-shaping experiences, including a divorce. Me? I've been through my own storms too, minus the divorce, because I have never been married. THANK GOD!!!!!! But trust, the lessons still came whether I signed papers or not.

She's a whole mama out here with four kids, two girls and two boys, and they're practically grown. Her youngest is 12. Meanwhile, I've got two; my oldest is 19, and my baby is 6. Yes… I started over again. And all I can say is DAMMIT!!!

But through every obstacle, every heartbreak, every period of distance, our bond never broke. It stretched, it bent, but it never snapped. We are, and always have been, inseparable in the ways that actually matter.

She talks about moving back to Georgia, and I want that more than anything, but she's a mom first. And I respect that. Still, let's be clear… that don't mean she can't get "flewed" out to see her bestie every now and then.

And let me say this, because it deserves its moment, my girl has been celibate for 7 months at the time of writing this book. So yes, go ahead and clap it up for her. Cheer her on. Encourage her to keep putting herself first.

Me, on the other hand? I'm currently going through it, bitch… send help!!!!

With all that distance between us, our phone calls have become something sacred. Real talk, they're therapy for the soul. No judgment, no filters, just truth, laughter, healing, and sometimes pure foolishness.

One day, Honey said, "We should write a book about the stuff we talk about on these calls." And just like that… here we are. What you're holding is a piece of those conversations, raw, real, and straight from us to you.

Now, between us, we call this whole experience "Wading in the Water." But out of respect, we didn't name the book that. That phrase comes from something much deeper, something sacred to our ancestors who endured and survived so much. We would never play with that.

But we do want you to know, if you ever hear us say "wading in the water" in future videos or conversations, now you know exactly what it means. No disrespect. Just an inside joke between two women of color who have been through life together and are still standing, still laughing, and still healing side by side, no matter the distance.

$$Hey girl,$$

I bet you thought this book was going to
be classy, didn't you? And it is... at least
on the pink pages.

But on the black pages? We 'bout to
turn up and get ratchet! Welcome to
the dark side.

Table of Contents

Before we get to
the nitty-gritty...

Let's talk facts.

Science

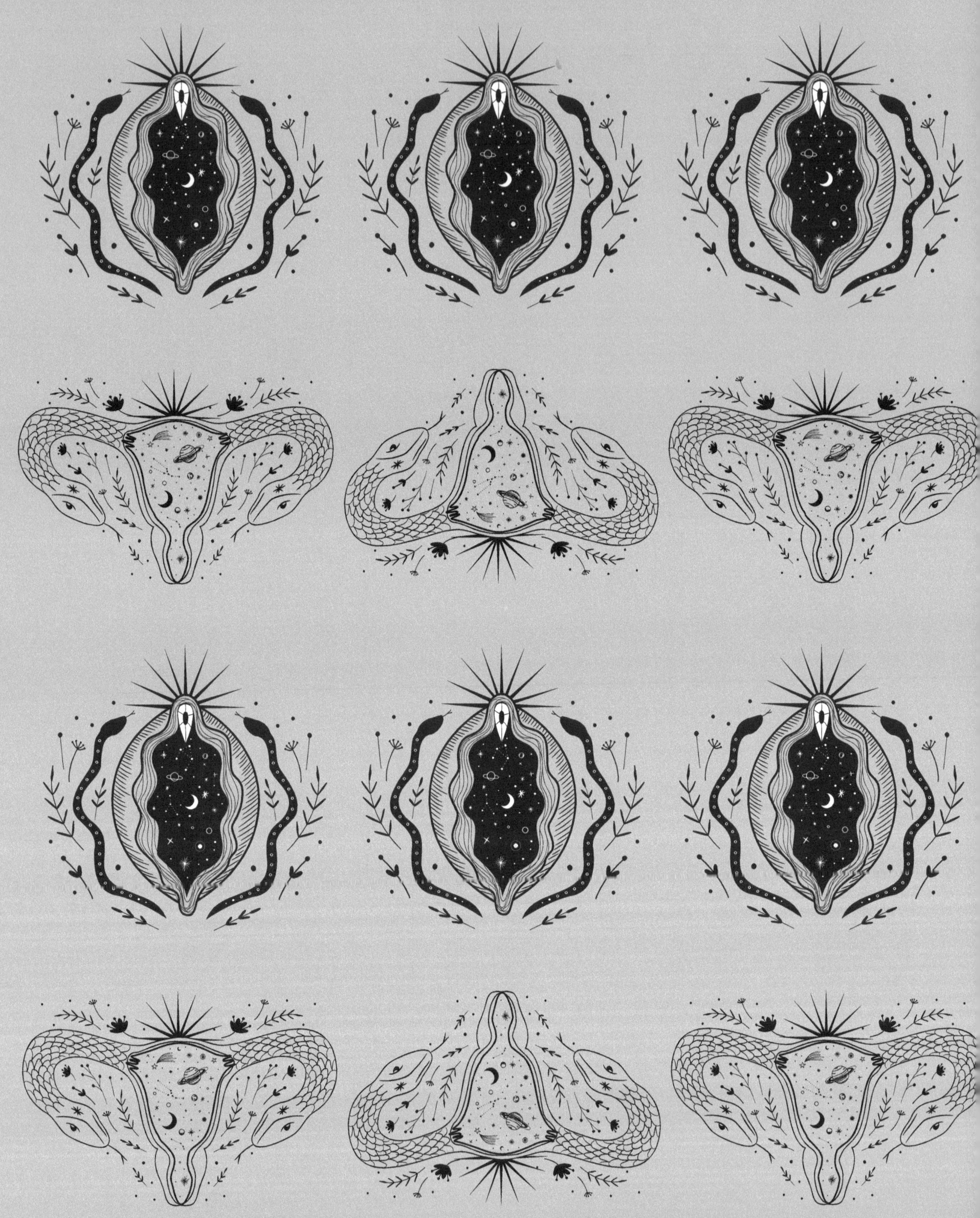

Ok bestie,
let's get to know your girl a little better.

This is your vagina.

The Outside (Vulva)

Mons Pubis
The soft, padded area that protects your pelvic bone.

Labia Majora (Outer lips)
The thicker outer lips that protect everything inside.

Labia Minora (Inner lips)
The inner lips are more sensitive and delicate. They swell when you're turned on.

Clitoris
Your pleasure center. She has thousands of nerve endings. And, her only job? Feeling good. That's it!

Urethra Opening
Where pee comes out. Tiny, and separate from everything else.

Vaginal Opening
The entrance to the vagina. This is where penetration happens and where blood exits during your cycle.

The Inside

Vagina
The internal canal. It stretches, expands, and cleans itself. She is low-maintenance, so don't go messing her up with harsh products.

Cervix
The doorway between your vagina and uterus. It opens slightly during ovulation and more during childbirth.

Uterus (Womb)
Where a baby would grow if you choose that path. Every month, it builds a lining and sheds it (your period) if no pregnancy happens.

Fallopian Tubes
Tiny pathways that carry eggs from your ovaries to your uterus.

Ovaries
These are your egg producers and hormone bosses. They release eggs and control estrogen & progesterone.

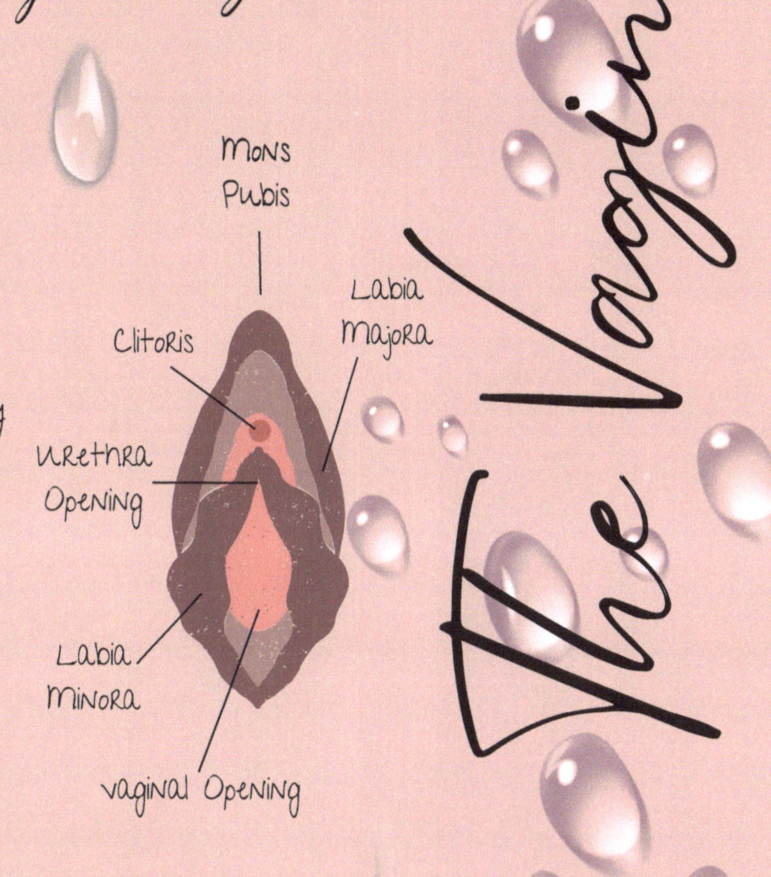

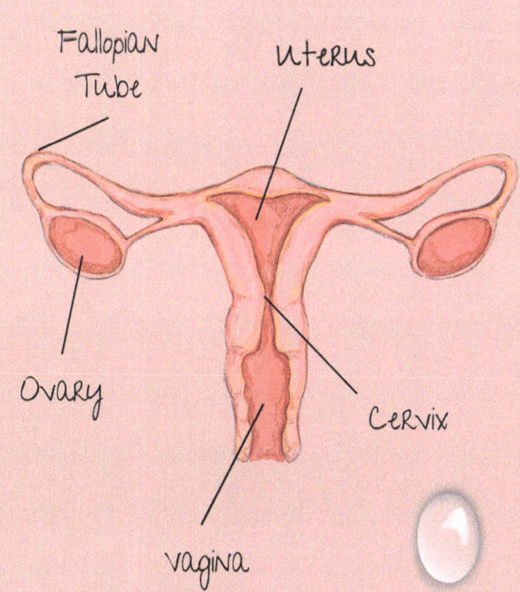

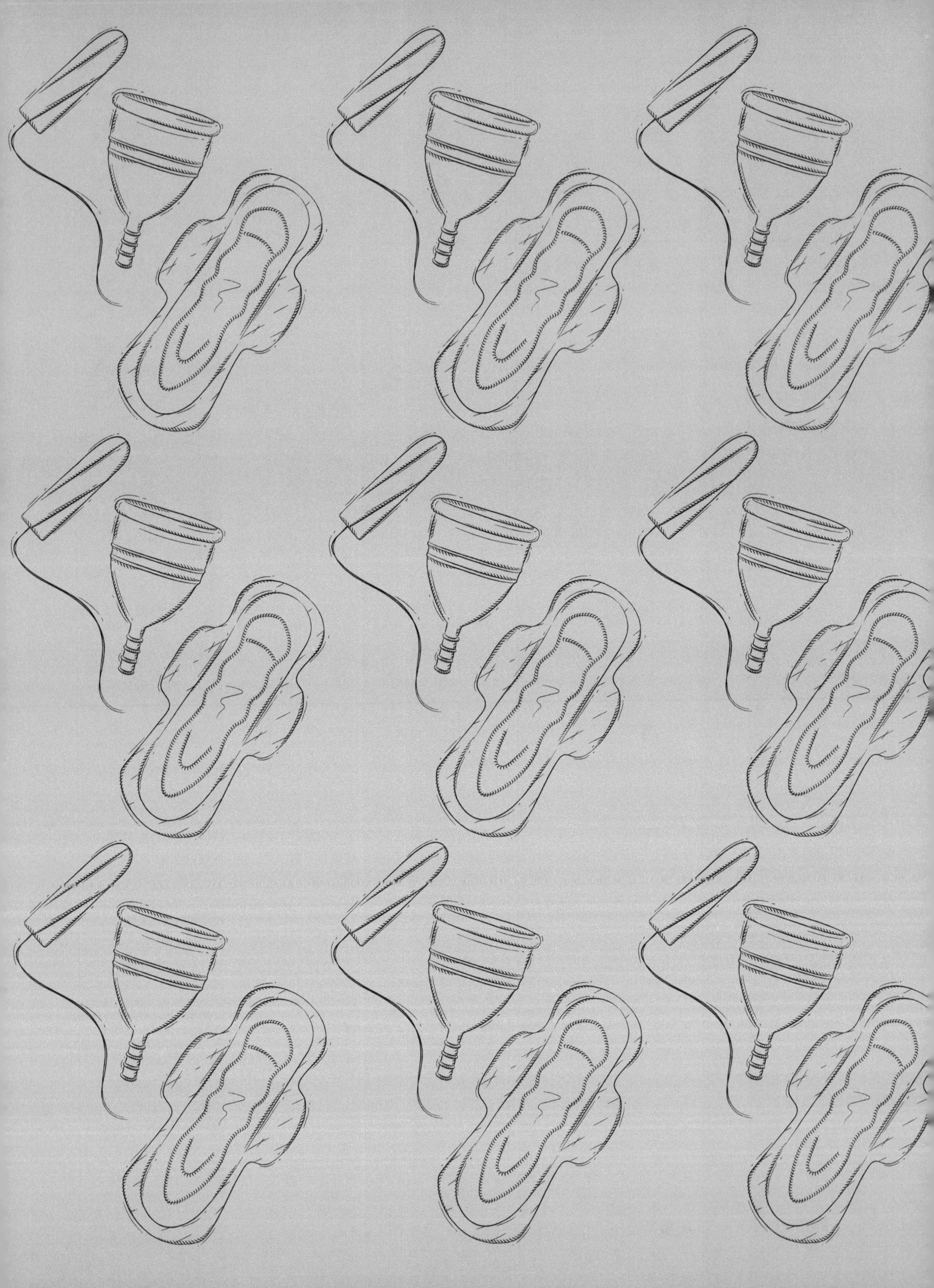

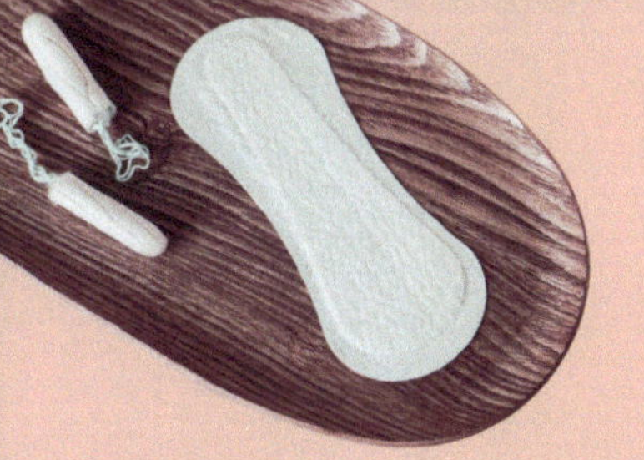

Your Cycle at a Glance

Your cycle is a monthly rhythm that comes every 21-35 days

1. Menstrual Phase (Your Period)

- The uterus sheds its lining (lasts about 3-7 days).
- Prostaglandins cause uterine contractions and shedding.

2. Follicular Phase (Rebuild Mode)

- Starts during your period and continues after.
- Your body begins preparing a new egg.
- Estrogen increases to thicken the uterine lining.

3. Ovulation (Peak Fertility Window)

- Your ovary releases an egg.
- The fertility window is usually 10 to 17 days after your period.
- You may notice changes in discharge (clear, stretchy).

4. Luteal Phase (Wind Down)

- Progesterone rises.
- Your body prepares for possible pregnancy.
- If no pregnancy occurs, your hormones drop & your period begins again.

Things to Know

Blood amount

- You only lose usually about 60 milliliters (around 2.7 ounces) of blood per cycle on average.

Color changes

- Bright red → fresh flow
- Pink/red → blood diluted by cervical fluid
- Dark red/brown → oxidized, slow-moving, or older blood
- Color changes are normal unless paired with a strong odor or pain.

Your cycle is a health signal and can tell you things about:

- Stress levels
- Diet
- Hormonal balance
- Overall health

Hormone shifts can affect:

- Mood
- Energy
- Libido

Wait ya'll , we have a pregnant woman in the house..

Say what? How do you think she got like that? Eeeooowww!!!

Libido During Pregnancy

Your sex drive during pregnancy can be... unpredictable.

First Trimester (Weeks 1-12)

- The first trimester is notorious for causing nausea, fatigue, breast tenderness, & mood swings.
- Your libido may drop.

Second Trimester (Weeks 13-28)

- You may regain your energy.
- Increased blood flow to the pelvic area may cause a higher libido and easier arousal.

Third Trimester (Weeks 29-birth)

- Libido may decrease due to physical discomfort, abdominal size, and fatigue.
- Your natural lubrication may increase.

Orgasms During Pregnancy

For many women:

- Orgasms can feel stronger or fuller.
- For most healthy pregnancies, sex & frequent orgasms are completely safe.

Sex Dreams During Pregnancy

- Do not be surprised if your dreams get a little more sexual during pregnancy. Hormones are shifting, blood flow is increased, and your body is more sensitive, so your mind may start expressing all of that in your dreams.
- Sex dreams are often connected to attraction, but they are not limited by it. They can involve almost anyone, regardless of your conscious feelings.

Emotional Side of Desire

- During pregnancy, some women feel more confident, others may feel self-conscious or detached. Either way, remember that you are a fierce queen and pregnancy is only temporary. Thank goodness.

Feed her right and she'll treat you right.

Supplements

Probiotic supplements
- Helps maintain vaginal pH and yeast.

Cranberry (extract or capsules)
- Often used for urinary tract health.

Omega-3 fatty acids
- Helps reduce inflammation & may increase vaginal lubrication.

Omega-7 fatty acids
- May relieve symptoms of menopause and dryness.

Prebiotics (the food for good bacteria)
- Feeds the healthy bacteria (like lactobacillus).
- Helps support the effectiveness of probiotics.

D-Mannose
- Helps prevent bacterial growth.

Curcumin with Black Pepper
- Has beneficial properties, including anti-inflammatory and antioxidant effects.

Caprylic Acid (from coconut oil)
- Has antifungal properties to help manage yeast.

Magnesium
- Helps with mood, hormone balance, & PMS symptoms.

B-Complex vitamins
- Supports energy, hormone regulation, & menstruation.

Evening Primrose Oil
- Supports hormonal balance, PMS symptoms, & breast tenderness.

Chasteberry (Vitex)
- Helps regulate hormones, irregular cycles, & PMS.

Plus Many More

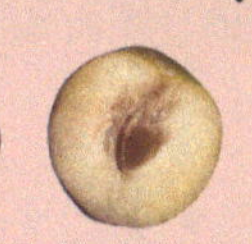

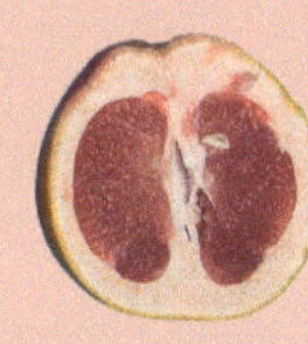

The Pussy Diet

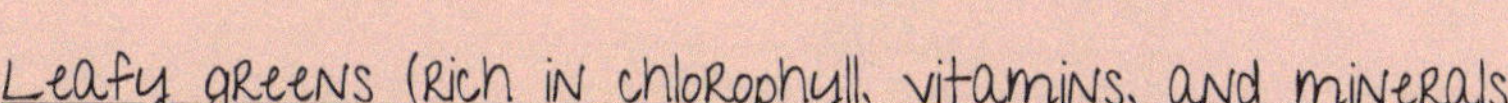

Leafy greens (rich in chlorophyll, vitamins, and minerals)
- Spinach
- Kale
- Collards

Probiotic-Rich foods (for good bacteria)
- Yogurt
- Kefir
- Sauerkraut
- Kimchi

Fruits (especially antioxidant-rich)
- Berries
- Apples
- Citrus fruits

Healthy fats
- Avocados
- Nuts
- Seeds
- Olive oil

Whole grains
- Oats
- Brown Rice
- Quinoa

Water
- Add okra for added natural lubrication.
- Helps your body flush toxins.

Popular Topical Remedies

Topical remedies are not clinically recommended, but if you intend to use these methods, please use caution:

- Tea Tree, Oregano, & other Essential Oils
- Boric Acid
- Garlic
- Yoni Pearls
- Vaginal Steam

BOXING
BOXING

Get it Right, Get it Tight!

Vaginal Exercises (Pelvic Floor Training)

Vaginal exercises are pelvic floor exercises that support the vagina, uterus, bladder, & bowel.

1. Kegels

How it's done:

- Using the same muscles you'd use to stop urine mid-stream,
  - tighten, hold for a few seconds, relax fully, & repeat.

Benefits:

- Improves bladder control.
- Supports pelvic health after childbirth.
- Increases awareness of pelvic muscles.
- Can enhance sensation for some women.

2. Reverse Kegels

How it's done:

Instead of tightening, you gently release and expand the pelvic floor muscles.

Benefits:

- Helps reduce pelvic tension.
- Balances over-tightened pelvic floors.
- Supports comfort during intimacy and daily life.

3. Pelvic Floor Breathing (Diaphragmatic Coordination)

How it's done:

- Inhale → pelvic floor relaxes.
- Exhale → pelvic floor gently engages.

Benefits:

- Reduces stress in the body.
- Improves mind-body connection.
- Supports overall pelvic health.

4. Functional Pelvic Engagement (During Movement)

Your pelvic floor naturally works during:

- Squats
- Core exercises
- Lifting

Caution: Overdoing Kegels can lead to:

- Tight pelvic floor muscles.
- Pain or discomfort.
- Reduced sexual pleasure for some women.
- Difficulty relaxing during intimacy or exams.

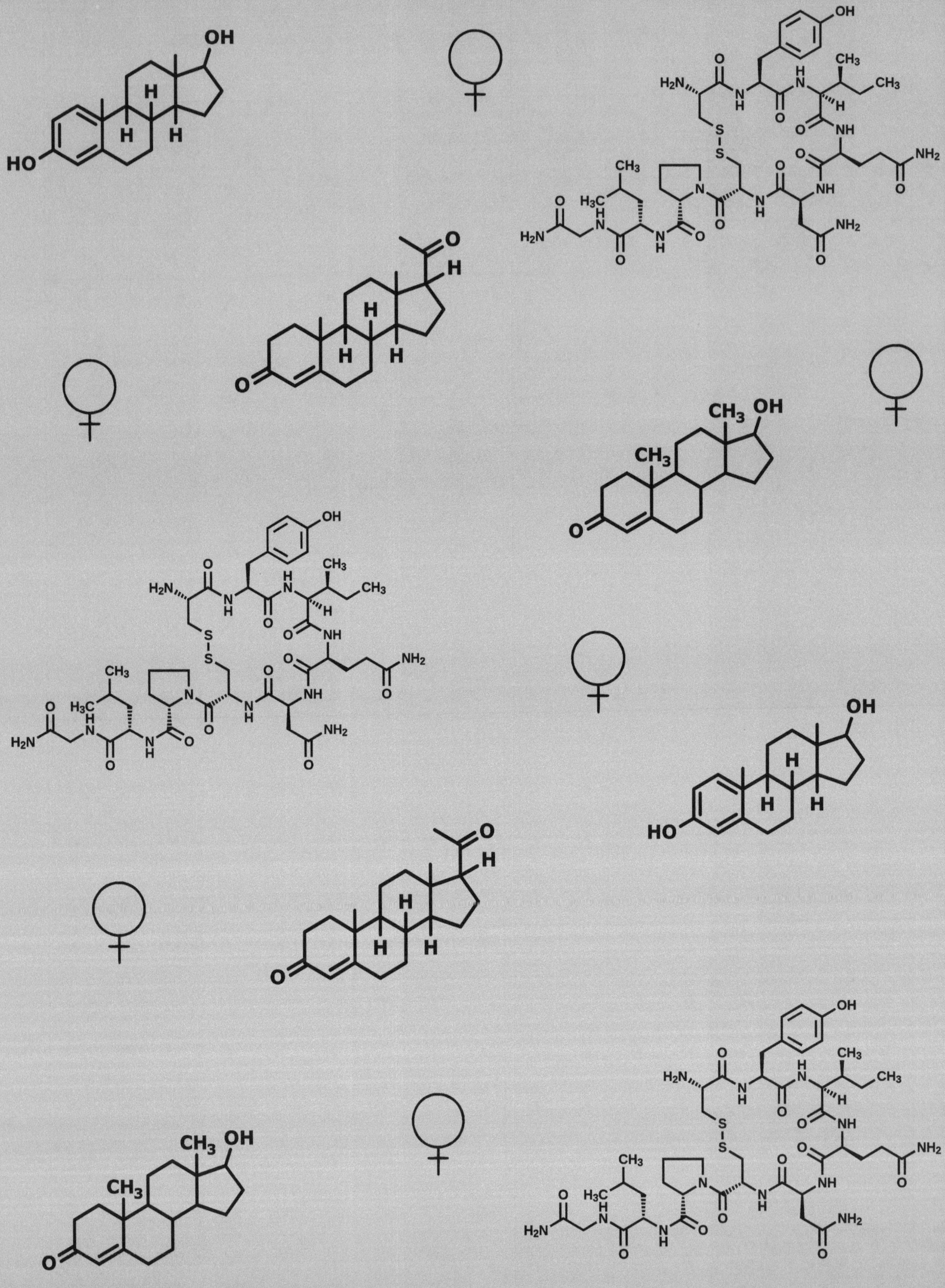

Why you gotta act like that?

Feminine Hormones

Hormones are your body's internal messaging system. They tell your brain, mood, cycle, libido, energy, and emotions what to do.
The main "big five" in the female body are:

1. Estrogen is your primary feminine hormone.
   What it does:
- Builds and regulates your menstrual cycle.
- Thickens the uterine lining each month.
- Supports skin & hair health & breast tissue.
- Influences mood, confidence, and social energy.
   How it can feel:
- More energetic.
- More social or flirty.
- Mentally sharp, especially in the follicular phase.

2. Progesterone shows up after ovulation.
   What it does:
- Stabilizes the uterine lining.
- Prepares the body for pregnancy.
- Slows things down physically and mentally.
   How it can feel:
- More calm or sleepy.
- More emotional or sensitive.
- Sometimes bloating or craving comfort.

3. Testosterone– Yes, women produce testosterone too
   What it does:
- Supports libido (sex drive).
- Affects motivation and confidence.
- Influences energy and physical drive.
   How it can feel:
- More desire or sexual interest.
- Promotes improved mood and mental health.
- Antidepressant effects.

4. hCG (Human Chorionic Gonadotropin)
   What it does:
- Signals pregnancy to the body.
- Maintains progesterone early on.
- Supports embryo development.
   How it can feel:
- Nausea.
- Extreme fatigue.
- Heightened smell sensitivity.

5. Oxytocin (The "Bonding Hormone")
- Released during touch, intimacy, childbirth, & nursing.
- Creates emotional bonding and trust.

The Hormone Cycle (How They Move Together)
- Period → hormones drop
- Follicular phase → estrogen rises
- Ovulation → estrogen peaks + testosterone rises
- Luteal phase → progesterone dominates
- Repeat

How Hormones Affect Libido
- When estrogen + testosterone rises, women may feel more desirable.
- When progesterone dominates, libido lowers & emotional intimacy needs increase.
- When stress (cortisol) increases, libido may shut down completely.

What is that smell?

Girl, it's me. I woke up like this.

What are Pheromones?

Pheromones are chemical substances that can influence the behavior and social responses of others within the same species. In humans, the primary compounds believed to act as pheromones include androstenone, androstenol, androstadienone, and estratetraenol. Among these, the following have shown particular significance in attracting males:

- Copulins → found in vaginal secretions, especially around ovulation. Copulins have implications for human mate choice, behavioral strategies, infertility, and sexual coercion (Williams & Jacobson, 2016).
- Estratetraenol (EST) → a compound related to estrogen, studied for scent signaling. Studies suggest that estratetraenol could increase men's sexual motivation, possibly facilitating behavioral processes associated with the pursuit of a sexual partner (Wu et al., 2022).

Now this is where it gets nuanced:
- Some studies show that when women are ovulating:
  - Men may rate them as more attractive.
  - Men's testosterone can increase slightly when exposed to it.

Where can you smell it the most?
- The vagina has a natural, unique scent that is influenced by hormones and pH levels, and it can subtly change throughout a woman's cycle, especially during ovulation.

Roses Really Smell Like...

Well, that is entirely up to you, my love.

Cleanliness is next to godliness.

Your vagina is naturally self-cleaning, so it doesn't need any internal washing. She keeps herself balanced by producing natural fluids that gently flush out dead cells, bacteria, and anything she doesn't need. On top of that, she's powered by good bacteria (lactobacillus) that help maintain a healthy, slightly acidic environment to protect you.

How to Take Care of Her
Outside (vulva)
- Wash with warm water.
- If you use soap, keep it mild & unscented.
- Gently clean between folds.

Inside (vagina)
- Leave her alone!
- No washing, no harsh products.

What NOT to Use:
- Douches!
- Scented soaps or body washes.
- Feminine sprays or perfumes.
- Wipes with fragrance or alcohol.
- Harsh antibacterial soaps.

All of these can:
- Throw off your pH.
- Kill good bacteria.
- Lead to irritation or infections.

What can safely support vaginal health?
- Plain, unscented products only for external use.
- Cotton underwear (lets her breathe).
- Staying dry.
- Balanced diet + hydration.

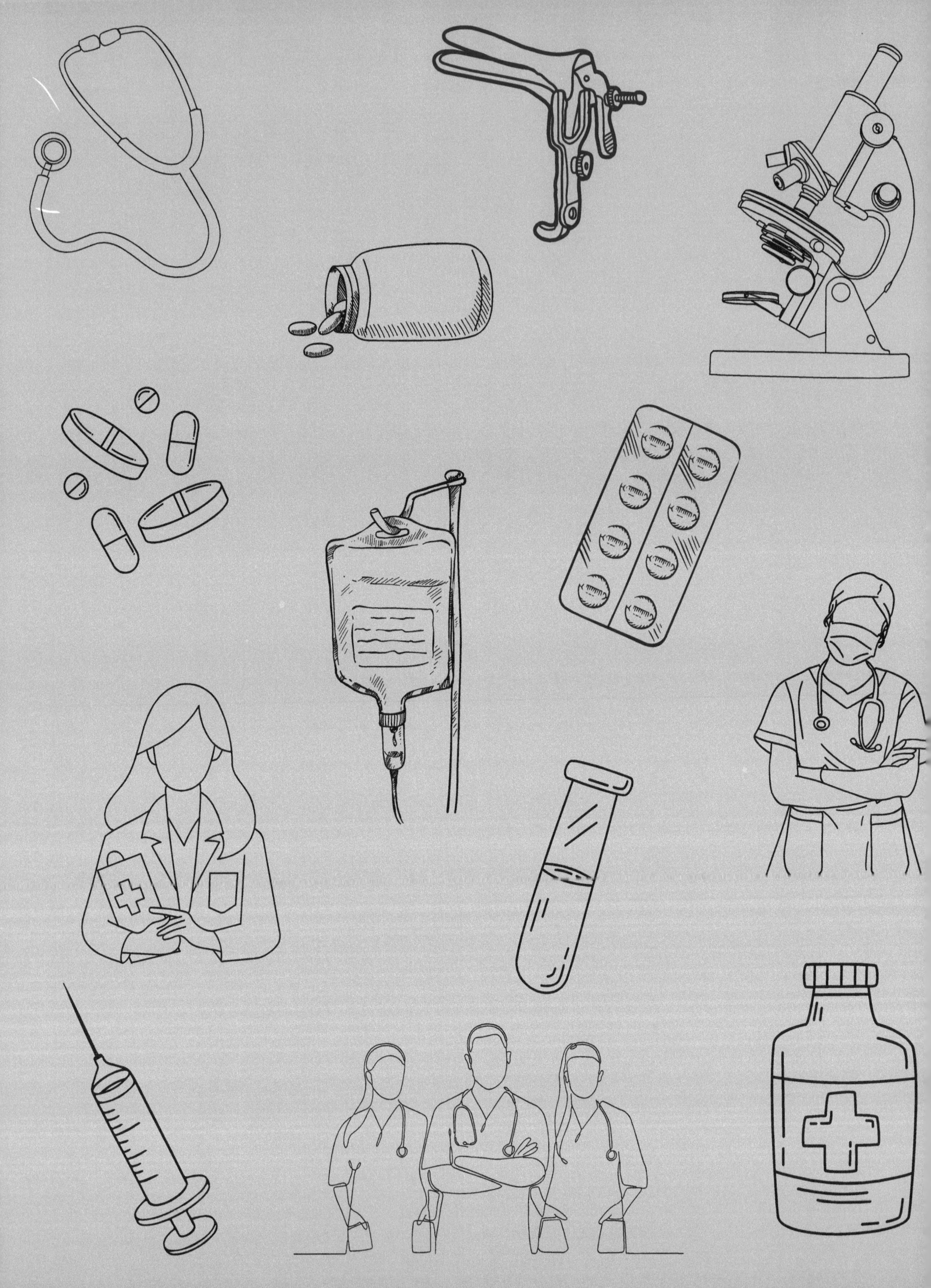

Ass Down, Legs Up...

That's the way you get checked up.

Common Gynecological Procedures

Breast Exam
What they do:
- Gently feel your breasts and underarm area.
- They check for lumps, changes, or anything unusual.

Pelvic Exam
External exam:
- They look at the vulva to check for irritation, swelling, or abnormalities.

Internal exam (with a speculum)
- It gently opens the vaginal walls so they can check for abnormalities inside the vaginal canal.

Pap Smear (Cervical Screening)
What it is:
- A small sample of cells taken from your cervix.

What it checks for:
- Early signs of cervical changes.
- Screens for cervical cancer.

STI Testing
How:
- A culture swab is taken during pelvic exam.
- A urine/blood test may be needed as well.

Bimanual Exam
The doctor:
- Inserts one or two gloved fingers inside the vaginal canal.
- Presses gently on your abdomen with the other hand.

Why:
- To feel the uterus and ovaries to check for size, shape, or tenderness.

Other Tests
Depending on your needs:
- Pregnancy test.
- Ultrasound (if something needs a closer look).
- Hormone testing (via bloodwork).

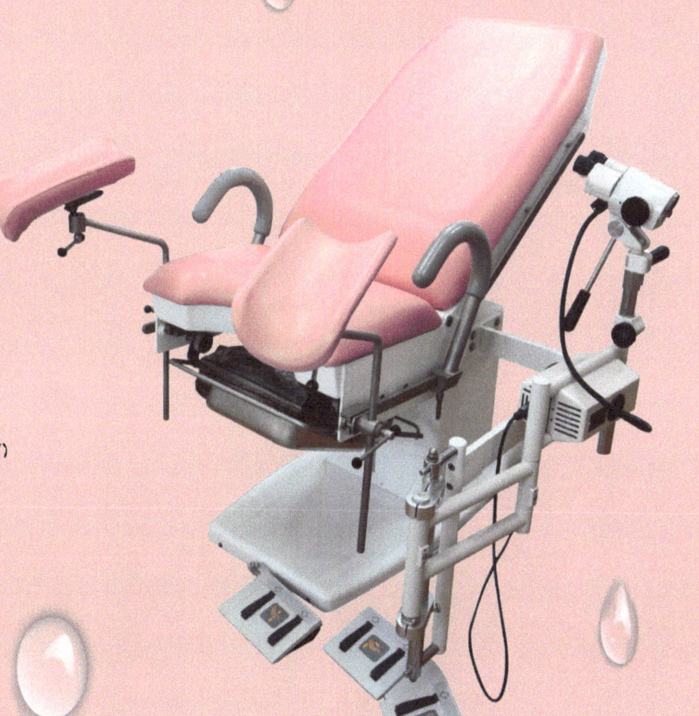

Types of feminine diseases

Polycystic Ovary Syndrome (PCOS)

A hormonal condition where the ovaries produce higher levels of androgens.

Common signs:

- Irregular or missed periods.
- Acne or oily skin.
- Excess hair growth (face, chest, etc.).
- Difficulty losing weight.
- Ovarian cysts.

Uterine Fibroids

Non-cancerous growths in or around the uterus.

Common signs:

- Heavy prolonged periods.
- Pelvic pressure or pain.
- Frequent urination (if pressing on the bladder).

Endometriosis

A tissue similar to the uterine lining that grows outside the uterus.

Common signs:

- Severe period pain.
- Pain during intimacy.
- Heavy bleeding.
- Fertility challenges.

Ovarian Cysts

Fluid-filled sacs that grow on the ovaries.

Common signs:

- Dull or sharp pain on the side of cyst.
- Pelvic pain, pressure, or bloating.
- Severe pain if one ruptures.

Menorrhagia (Heavy menstrual bleeding)

Abnormally heavy or prolonged periods.

Common signs:

- Bleeding through products quickly.
- Periods lasting longer than 7 days.
- Fatigue (possible anemia).

Adenomyosis

When the uterine lining grows into the muscle of the uterus.

Common signs:

- Very heavy, painful periods.
- Pelvic pressure by an enlarged uterus.

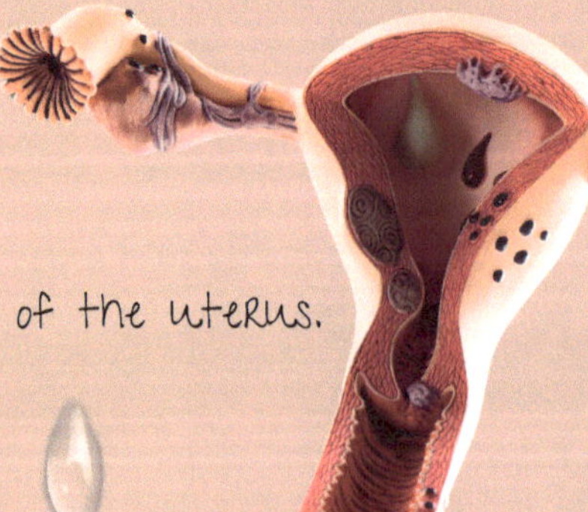

Types of feminine diseases continued

Premenstrual Dysphoric Disorder (PMDD)
A severe form of PMS that affects mood and mental health.
Common Signs:

- Intense mood swings.
- Depression or anxiety before your period.
- Irritability that feels out of character.

Pelvic Inflammatory Disease (PID)
An infection of the reproductive organs, often from untreated STIs.
Common Signs:

- Lower abdominal pain.
- Fever & Nausea.
- Unusual foul-smelling discharge.
- Pain during intimacy.

Vaginismus
Involuntary tightening of vaginal muscles that makes penetration painful or difficult.
Common Signs:

- Pain with insertion (tampons, exams, intimacy).
- Muscle tightening you can't control.

Lichen sclerosus
A chronic skin condition affecting the vulva.
Common Signs:

- Itching.
- Thin, white patches of skin.
- Discomfort or tearing.

Vulvodynia
Chronic vulvar pain with no clear cause.
Common Signs:

- Burning, stinging, or irritation.
- Pain with touch or pressure.

Amenorrhea
Missing periods (not due to pregnancy).
Causes can include:

- Stress.
- Weight changes.
- Hormonal imbalance.
- Intense exercise.

Types of STIs

Sexually Transmitted Infections (STIs)

These are infections passed through sexual contact.

Chlamydia
- Pain or discomfort in the lower abdomen.
- Can cause discharge or pain when urinating.
- Treatable with antibiotics.

Gonorrhea
- Vaginal discharge & bleeding during intercourse.
- Causes pain or burning when urinating.
- Treatable with antibiotics.

Human Papillomavirus (HPV)
- Some types cause genital warts.
- Some types are linked to cervical cancer.
- Vaccines help protect against infections & cancer.

Herpes Simplex Virus (HSV)
- Causes periodic outbreaks (sores/blisters).
- Stays in the body but can be managed.

Bacterial Vaginosis (BV)
- Caused by an imbalance of vaginal bacteria.
- Causes discharge with a strong odor.
- Treatable with antibiotics.

Yeast Infection
- Overgrowth of yeast.
- Causes vaginal itching, soreness, and discharge.
- Treated with antifungal medications.

Trichomoniasis ("Trich")
- A very common STI caused by a parasite.
- Causes unusual foul-smelling discharge.
- Itching, burning, redness or soreness of the genitals.
- Discomfort when peeing.
- Treatable with medication.

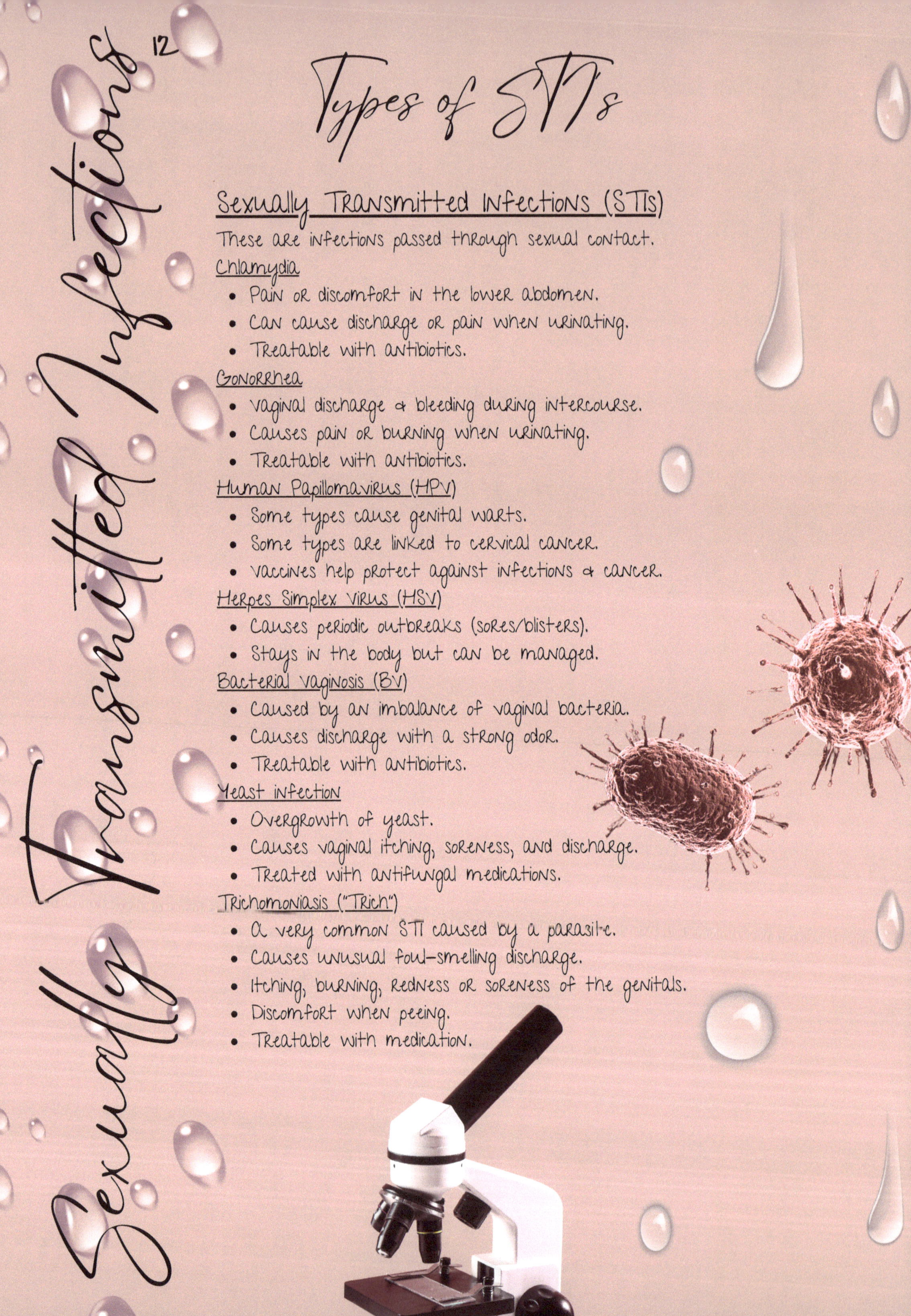

Types of STIs
continued

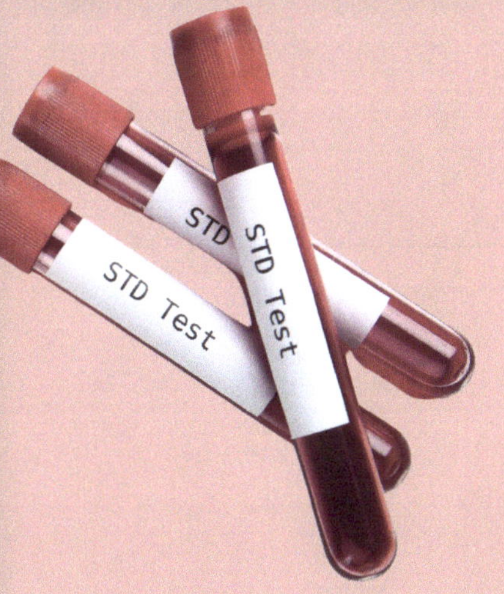

<u>Hepatitis B</u>
- A virus that affects the liver.
- Causes jaundice & dark urine.
- Causes fatigue, nausea, & vomiting.
- Chronic condition that requires ongoing medication.

<u>Hepatitis C</u>
- A virus that affects the liver.
- Causes jaundice & dark urine.
- Causes fatigue, fever, nausea, & vomiting.
- There is a curable oral treatment available.

<u>Syphilis</u>
- A bacterial infection that progresses in stages.
- Painless sores (early stage).
- Rash on the body (later stage).
- Serious complications if untreated.
- Treatable with antibiotics.

<u>Human immunodeficiency virus (HIV)</u>
- A virus that affects the immune system.
- Flu-like symptoms (early stage)
- Weakened immune system (later stage)
- Chronic condition that requires ongoing medication.

<u>Mycoplasma genitalium</u>
- Can infect the cervix.
- Causes vaginal discharge.
- Causes burning when urinating.
- Treatable with antibiotics.

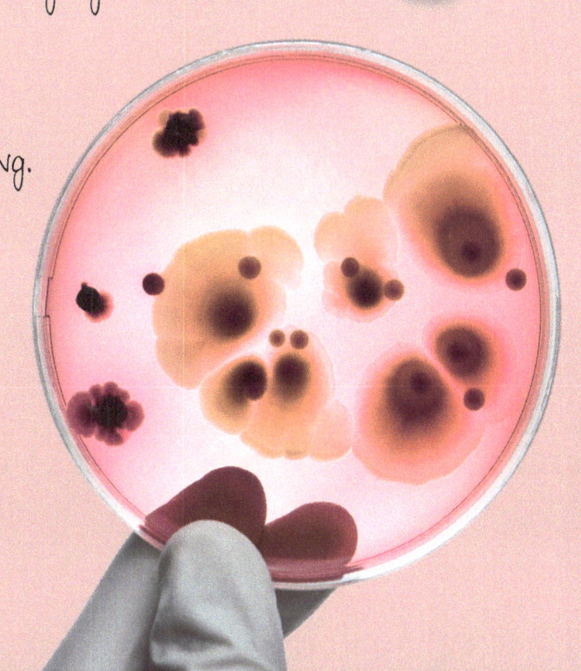

Sexually Transmitted Infections

XOXO

The G Spot

Be honest... how many of you reading this have actually experienced an orgasm from penetration alone? Now, for those of you saying yes—okay, I hear you. But let me ask you this... was it from a man? Girl. Be serious. Oh, it was? And does he have a brother? Asking for the group. Because let's not lie to ourselves, some of these men are out here struggling to find the very obvious "on" button. So how exactly are they supposed to locate the G spot, which sits on the front wall, about one to two inches inside? Exactly.

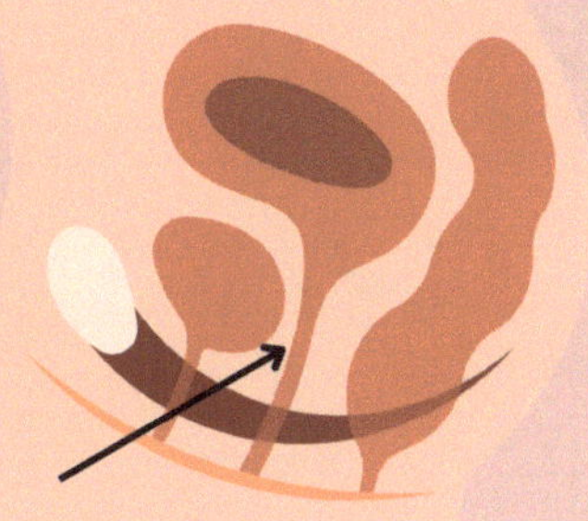

The Nipples

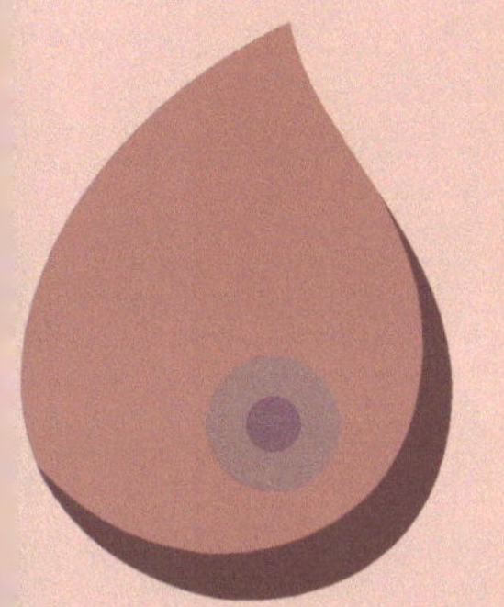

Ahh, the nipples... those sensitive little chocolate drops that can send chills down your spine and, under the right circumstances, echo that sensation all the way to the clitoris.

The Clitoris

All rise for the queen of all queens, the reason so many women truly enjoy sex, and quite possibly the reason we have not all lost our minds from stress... the clitoris. It takes one powerful woman to center her own pleasure and honor it without apology. Can we get a round of applause?

Other Erogenous Zones

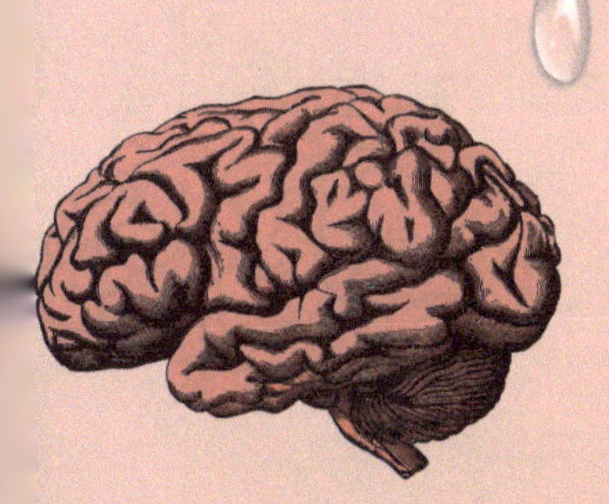

The neck, lips, thighs, and other areas that respond to touch are all examples of arousal zones. But ladies, we are forgetting one very important one. Do you know which one? The mind. Yes. This one may be the most powerful of them all. When you learn to listen to yourself and trust your intuition, it will rarely lead you astray.

RIP
Taj Mahal

Pussy will have 'em...

- Starting wars (The Trojan War)
- Renouncing their crown (King Edward VIII)
- Building monuments (Taj Mahal)
- Or even killing themselves (Story of Cleopatra)

The importance of sexual safety

<u>Protect your throne by staying proactive and prioritizing prevention.</u>

First and foremost, dirty 👏 dick 👏 will 👏 mess 👏 up 👏 your:

- potential of Hydrogen (pH) levels.
- vaginal microbiome
- smell
- homeostasis
- health and livelihood
- sanity

Please consider using female condoms!

<u>To protect yourself from sexual violence, consider:</u>

- Learning self-defense.
- Practicing situational awareness.
- Carrying personal safety tools that are legal in your area.
- Practicing becoming a gray woman or hiding in plain sight.
  – i.e., clothing, your scent, voice, and physical appearance.
- Wearing rape-proof gear such as a chastity belt. No, I am not joking. Modern ones are available online.
- Being creative— Protect yourself by any means necessary. But it is also important to understand the reality of the legal system. In some situations, women who defend themselves can still face serious legal consequences depending on how the law is applied. So no, do not be a victim. Your safety is a priority. But move with awareness. I cannot tell you what to do, but I can tell you there are many ways to protect yourself, and the goal is to choose methods that keep you safe now and protected in the long run.

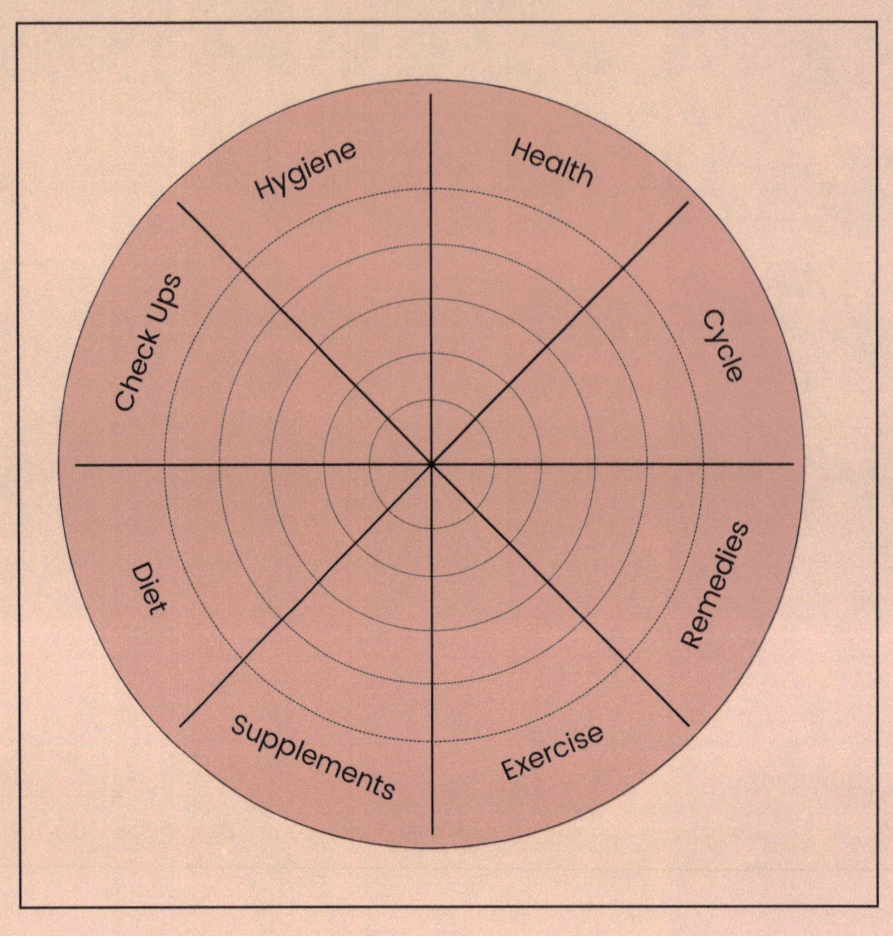

Affirmations for Sexual Liberation & Feminine Power

- I honor my body as a source of wisdom, pleasure, and power.
- I release shame and fully embrace my sensual, authentic self.
- My femininity is fluid, radiant, and uniquely mine.
- I choose connection that honors my body, mind, and spirit.
- I trust myself to set boundaries that protect my peace and pleasure.
- I reclaim every part of myself that I was taught to suppress.
- My pleasure is not a luxury—it is a birthright.
- I am worthy of deep intimacy, starting with myself.
- I am safe to be fully expressed in my femininity.
- I release guilt around being seen, desired, and expressed.
- I deserve pleasure, presence, and partners who meet me with intention.

Self Love Reminder

Notes

Pleasure

Now , let the fun begin!

Within these dark pages of bliss, we are going to explore all the different ways to pleasure yourself. Now, before we get into it, do not come for me and start judging me like I am the only one who has ever tried any of the things we are about to talk about. Okay?

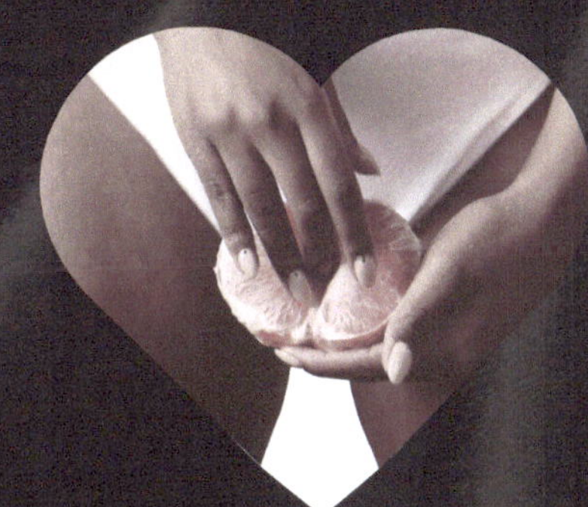

Feel the Vibe...
Literally.

Clitoral Stimulators
Common types:

- Vibrators → provides steady or pulsing vibration.
- Air-pulse → creates waves of air pressure without direct contact.
- Suction-Style → creates a gentle seal to produce a rhythmic vacuum sensation.

Vaginal Penetrators
Common types:

- Classic vibrators → smooth or ribbed, straight or slightly curved.
- Curved/internal stimulators → designed to reach sensitive internal areas.
- Non-vibrating options → for those who prefer pressure over vibration.

Dual-Stimulation Toys
Combine two or more of the following:

- Clitoral stimulation
- Vaginal penetration
- Anal stimulation and/or penetration.

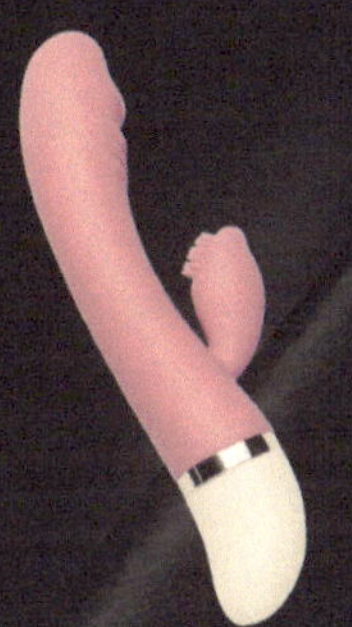

Anal Options
Common types:

- Plugs → tapered for easier insertion, with a flared base for safety.
- Beads → a string of multiple rounded segments.

Safety Rules:

- ALWAYS use toys with a flared base.
- Use plenty of lubrication.
- Go slow & be careful because this area does not self-lubricate.

Nipple Stimulators
These focus on the breasts and nipples, which can be very sensitive for some women.
Common types:

- Suction stimulators → create a gentle pulling sensation.
- Nipple Clamps → tailors the intensity of a squeezing sensation.
- Vibrating options → add sensation through vibration.

Ooooohh, you nasty.

Hey, Ain't No shame. I'm just saying the quiet part out loud.

Now, we have all been there. Curious and horny as hell. Looking around at everyday objects like they might be the answer to an itch you just cannot quite reach. Sitting there wondering... how strong is the vibration on my phone? Or what would this vibrating game controller feel like if I placed it right there? We all have intrusive thoughts. The only thing that separates the freaks from the conservatives is acting on those impulses. Okay, wait... pause. Because Now y'all starting to scare me a little. There is such a thing as going too far. And while most of us have some common sense... a few of y'all are out here getting a little too creative. Girl. Be calm.

This is Not the time to be turning your house into a damn science experiment. The goal is to have fun and handle your business, not end up googling "how to explain this to a doctor" at 2 a.m. Yes, be adventurous. Yes, explore. But also... be safe, be gentle, and please do Not do anything that would have you sitting there like, "Now how did I even get myself into this situation?"

I will neither confirm nor deny that I have either thought about or have tried any of the following items as Unconventional Clitoral Stimulators:

- Electric Toothbrushes
- Cell Phones
- Game Controllers
- Personal Massagers

As for Unconventional Penetrators? Girl, No. My level of freak stops here. And let me be real, I do not need to spell everything out. I trust you to get creative and handle your business. Just... be safe and make smart choices, because I am not coming to save you. And, you better not tell them that I told you to do it. Ya nasty.

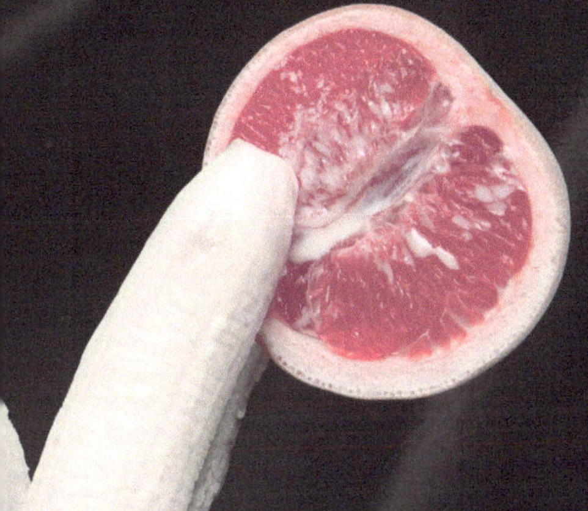

How did she do that?

And can she teach me how?

What Is a "Coregasm"?

Exercise-induced arousal (EIA) and exercise-induced orgasm (EIO) have been described as occurring from engaging in exercise or physical activities that are vigorous, repetitive, or demanding of core abdominal muscles, usually apart from sexual situations and without direct genital stimulation. (Herbenick, et al., 2025)

Why It Might Happen (The Science Behind It)

Researchers and clinicians suggest a few possible mechanisms:

1. Pelvic floor muscle activation through intense contraction.

2. Abdominal + strong core activation increases pressure in the pelvic region.

3. The pudendal nerve and surrounding pelvic nerves are involved in both exercise sensation and sexual response.

4. Exercise increases blood flow throughout the pelvis.

Exercises Some Women Report As Triggers

1. Abdominal crunches / sit-ups

2. Hanging leg raises on the Captain's chair

3. Yoga & meditation:

- Warrior pose
- Leg bicycles while holding V posture
- The combination of breath + muscle engagement

4. Cycling / stationary bike

5. Climbing / pull-ups

6. Heavy compound lifting

7. Elliptical / Treadmill / stair machines

8. Gymnastics

9. Carnival rides or swings

10. Horseback riding & motorcycle riding

Important Reality Check

- Only a small percentage of women report this experience.
- It's more like a neurological coincidence than a reproducible skill.
- Trying to "force it" can lead to:
  - Discomfort
  - Pelvic floor strain
  - Mental frustration

Why It Happens More in Some People

- Stronger pelvic floor muscles
- Higher body awareness
- Nerve sensitivity differences
- Hormonal state (ovulation may increase sensitivity)
- Relaxed psychological state during exercise

Ain't no better feeling than the touch of a human being.

Especially if it's coming from a fine ass man who knows what he's doing!

The touch of another person's body really is one of the most satisfying feelings in the world. The visuals, the sounds, the smells... whew. It's a full sensory experience. But let's be honest. In 2026? Girl... who actually has a man doing all that? Let me rephrase. Who has a man who is doing all that correctly? Actually, wait... one more time for the people in the back. Who has a man doing all that correctly without bringing along heartache or a headache? Exactly. It's ghetto out here.

But, in all seriousness, masturbation is a dying art, and a big part of that is due to modern technology. How are fingers supposed to compete with something that vibrates, pulsates, and penetrates all at the same time? Now we out here overstimulated, desensitized, and finishing faster than a microwave minute. And it's all because of that little "Rose" you swear you don't have... but it is definitely in your bedside drawer right now, fully charged. Don't look at me like that. I know.

So here is my invitation to you: discipline yourself. Take a step back for a while. Give yourself space from constant stimulation so you can reset. And when you come back, rediscover what it feels like to connect with your own body, without all the extra cheat codes. Just you, learning your rhythm again, and remembering that real fulfillment does not have to be rushed or outsourced.

Ok, I really wasn't buying that either. Go ahead. Grab that toy and go to town, girl. Gotta work smarter, not harder, I guess. Can't blame a girl for trying.

Human Touch

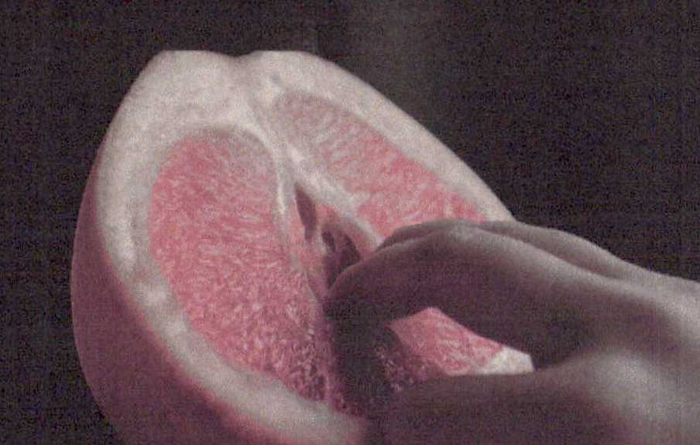

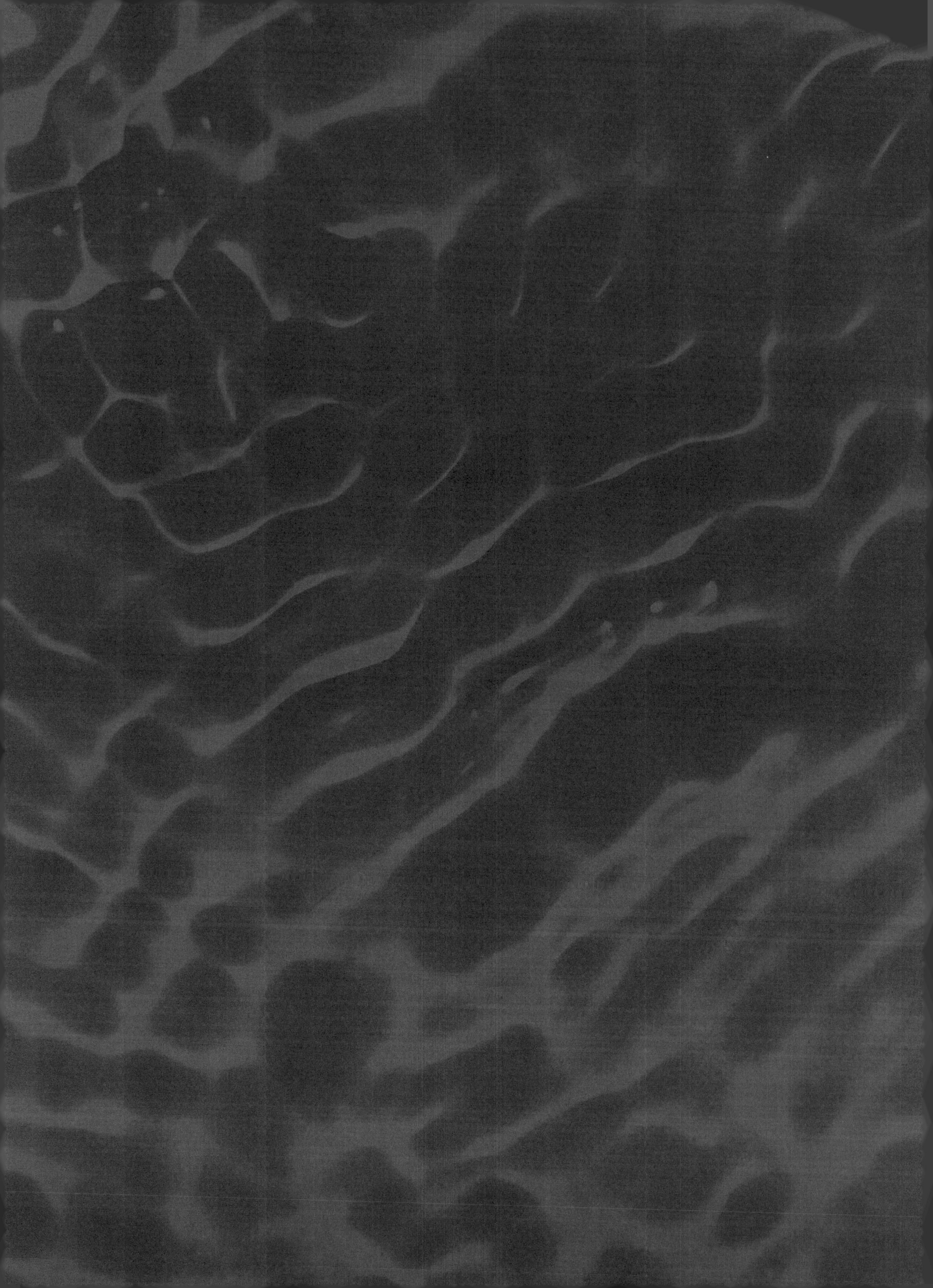

In the end , you always return to the water.

No matter where life takes you, you always circle back to what you know. And for many of us, the water was the first place we discovered what it really felt like to be a woman.

The Shower Head

The time a woman takes to clean herself is sacred. Take this time to focus on really cleaning your pleasure button. She cannot be ignored.

The Faucet

Go ahead and scoot down until your clitoris is positioned right under the flowing water. One word... Euphoric.

The Rain

Imagine it. You lying naked on a beautiful day, legs open and water droplets pouring right on your pleasure zone. Sounds therapeutic, doesn't it?

Water Hoses

Are you a gardener? Have you ever considered watering your own personal garden? Well, why not? Don't knock it 'til you try it.

Waterfalls

Don't listen to TLC. You better chase that waterfall and lie right underneath it. Spread eagle.

Hot Tub Jets

You know the relaxation you feel when you let the water from the jets massage your back. Now, turn around.

Sprinklers & Geysers

Stand over the shooting water and wiggle around until you feel something. What? If anyone asks, tell them you are just standing there minding your own business.

Bet you've never tried this before.

Positions*

Make It Rain

Stand comfortably in the shower and gently lift one leg, resting it on the edge of the tub or a stable surface. Let the water run all over your coochie while you just lean back into the vibe. Focus on your breathing and the sensation of the water cascading over your clitoris. This pose allows you to take control and experience that "climbing" feel with shower head kisses.

Face Down, Ass Up

Begin by lowering yourself carefully onto your hands and knees. From here, toot that thang up! Face down, ass up, and let it flow. Position your booty under the flowing water. Allow the water to find your clitoris and let the surrounding steam help soften tension in your shoulders and spine. Hold the position, breathe deeply, and surrender to the sensation of a clitoral massage.

Mimic A Lick

Sit or recline comfortably in the tub with the water running lightly. Allow your body to relax, letting your knees open like unfolding petals. Let the gentle water trickle from the shower onto your pussy. Place your hands on your thighs or gently massage your nipples. Focus on the rhythm of the water and your breathing. This is a moment for slowing down, releasing tension, and reconnecting with your body in a calm, supported way.

Bounce On It

Drop that thang like you are about to bounce and throw that ass in a circle. This is a playful kneeling pose hovering over a shower head that has been placed on the floor. Roll your hips in confident waves while the shower spray adds fluttering kisses upward to your pleasure button. This position encourages dominance, confidence, control, and a deeper awareness of your body's natural rhythm.

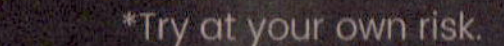

*Try at your own risk.

Wait, there's more...

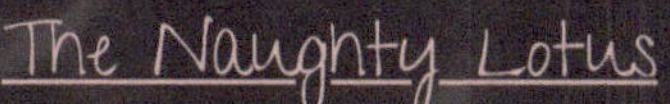

Do It With No Hands

Lie on your back and scoot your booty down until your coochie is positioned under the gentle stream of the tub faucet. Legs can be bent or extended against the wall for support. This hands-free option lets water do the work, allowing you to focus on breathing, touching other erogenous zones (nipples, inner thighs), or adding light manual stimulation. It's relaxing, powerful, and prioritizes surrender to sensation.

The Naughty Lotus

Sit cross-legged or in a butterfly position (soles of feet together, knees out) on the shower floor. This opens the hips and pelvis for easier access. Aim the shower head between your legs. Clench pelvic floor muscles rhythmically while the water flows and relax until an orgasm is achieved.

Buss It Wide Open *

Begin by facing the back wall. Stand with your feet grounded and your body steady. Shift your weight onto one leg, making sure you feel balanced on a non-slip surface. As the warm water flows over you, slowly hinge forward and lift your opposite leg behind you. Your hands can rest on the wall, the edge of the tub, or the floor for support. Focus on length rather than height, allowing your lifted leg to extend naturally. Let the steam soften your muscles as you breathe and find stability. Move your body slowly until the water hits the right pleasure spot and enjoy the pose while you maintain control and avoid slipping.

Twerk It

Stand with your feet set wide apart on a non-slip surface, making sure you feel stable before you begin. Bend over like you're about to back that ass up, allowing your upper body to fold down toward the floor. You can rest your hands on your thighs, the floor, or a stable surface for support. Let the warm water fall over your booty and roll down your coochie as you take a deep breath. Stay here for a few breaths, feeling the stretch deepen and the flow of water massage your magic bean.

Positions

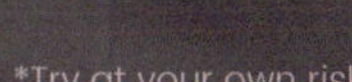

*Try at your own risk.

Thought we were done?

Positions*

Pussy Talk*

Begin by lying on your back on a stable, non-slip surface, with your knees bent and feet planted firmly about hip-width apart. Place your hands beside your ears with your fingers pointing toward your shoulders. Press evenly through your feet and hands as you slowly lift your hips and chest upward. Move with control, allowing your body to open gradually rather than forcing the position. Once stable, lift one of your legs and let the water trickle down your kitty.

Dickin-N-Drippin

This setting combines a dual sensation mimicking a ménage à trois. How, you may ask? Just add your favorite penetrating toy to any of these positions and ride the wave to a multi-layered symphony of sensation. Gyrate, twirl, or move it gently inside while the shower streams warmly over your yoni.

The Freaky Gemini

Focus the showerhead on your pussy. Take a few minutes under the warmth to unwind, then surprise yourself with a quick cool burst. Alternate the temperature while the water flows, trail your fingers lightly over your scalp, neck, inner arms, and thighs, all while letting the spray embrace every erogenous zone before focusing on your center. To add to your temperature experience, press your body against the cool wall while the water flows, letting your magic bean respond to the delicious hot-and-cold dance. Hot water, cold reality, zero regrets. I said what I said.

*Try at your own risk.

Relax and Release

More yoga poses for the adventurous, limber goddesses.

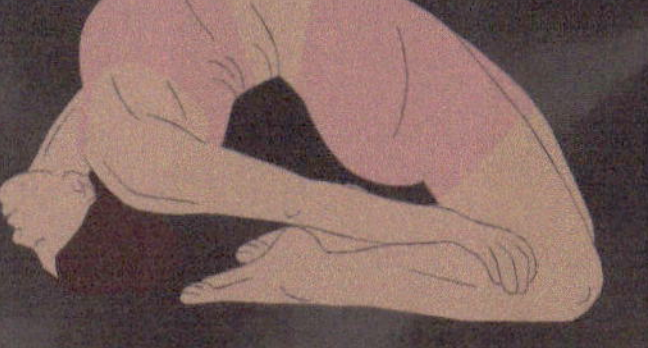
CRANE

Crescent Lunge

Downward-Facing Dog

Upward Plank

Heron

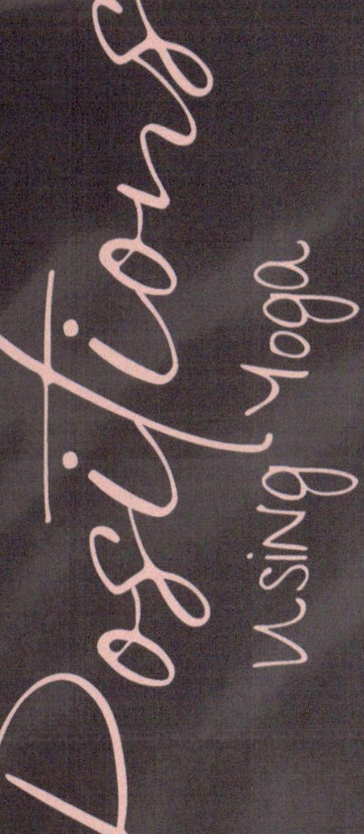

Little Thunderbolt

Supported Headstand

Seated Wheel

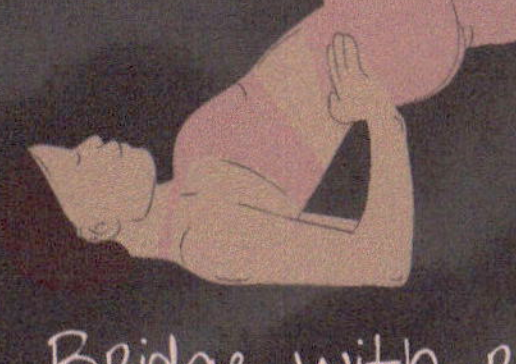
Bridge with raised leg

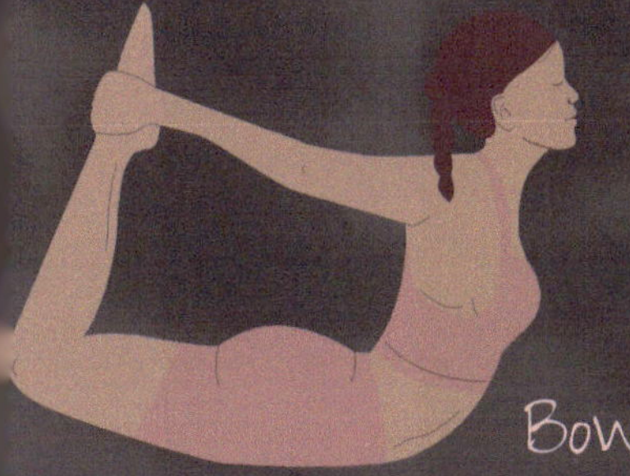
Bow

Scorpion

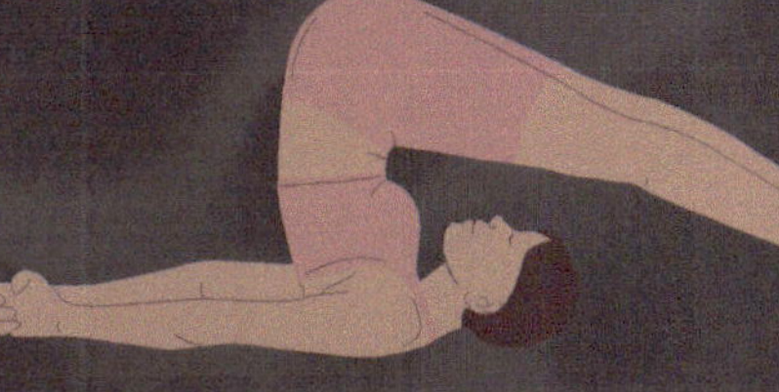
Plow

*Try at your own risk.

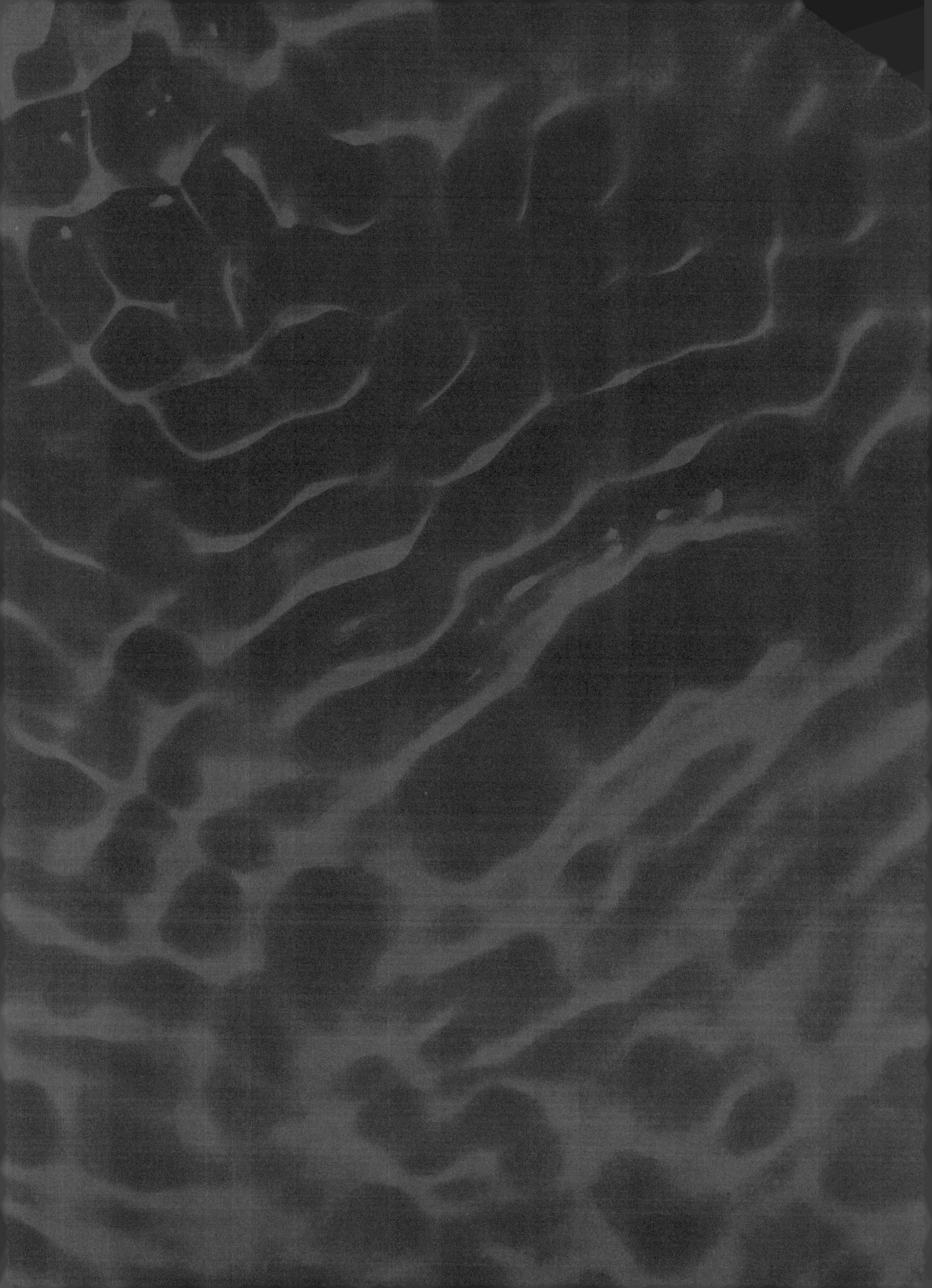

Thank you

Thank you for your purchase, your support, and for believing in the vision to help build a world full of sexually liberated, self-sufficient women who do not need rescuing because they already have everything within themselves to overcome whatever life throws their way.

This is bigger than a book. This is a mindset. A reclamation. A rebellion. Around here, we are not waiting to be chosen, saved, or completed. We are choosing ourselves fully, boldly, and without apology.

So no, you did not just buy a product.

You stepped into a movement.

Now, go forth and wade in the water, sis.

Welcome to the tribe!

Love ,

References

ACOG. (2018, March) Barrier Methods of Birth Control: Spermicide, Condom, Sponge, Diaphragm, and Cervical Cap. Www.acog.org.https://www.acog.org/womens-health/faqs/barrier-methods-of-birth-control-spermicide-condom-sponge-diaphragm-and-cervical-cap

Ajmera, R. (2021, March 10) 6 Vitamins That May Help with Vaginal Dryness. Healthline; Healthline Media. https://www.healthline.com/nutrition/vitamins-to-increase-female-lubrication#takeaway

Allshouse A, Pavlovic J, Santoro N. Menstrual Cycle Hormone Changes Associated with Reproductive Aging and How They May Relate to Symptoms. Obstet Gynecol Clin North Am. 2018 Dec;45(4)613-628. doi: 10.1016/j.ogc.2018.07.004. Epub 2018 Oct 25. PMID: 30401546; PMCID: PMC6226272.

CDC. (2024, May 7) Sexually Transmitted Infections (STIs) Sexually Transmitted Infections (STIs) https://www.cdc.gov/sti/index.html

Couri, M. (2022, March 28) 10 Important Supplements for Women's Health* - Couri Center. Couri Center. https://www.couricenter.com/articles/dr-couris-top-10-supplements-for-womens-health/

Değer MD, Akgul B. Global web trends analysis of sex toys. Sex Med. 2024 Nov 26;12(5)qfae072. doi: 10.1093/sexmed/qfae072. PMID: 39600963; PMCID: PMC11596685.

De Seta F, Lonnee-Hoffmann R, Campisciano G, Comar M, Verstraelen H, Vieira-Baptista P, Ventolini G, Lev-Sagie A. The Vaginal Microbiome: III. The Vaginal Microbiome in Various Urogenital Disorders. J Low Genit Tract Dis. 2022 Jan 1;26(1)85-92. doi: 10.1097/LGT.0000000000000645. PMID: 34928258; PMCID: PMC8719503.

d'Oro LC, Parazzini F, Naldi L, La Vecchia C. Barrier methods of contraception, spermicides, and sexually transmitted diseases: a review. Genitourin Med. 1994 Dec;70(6)410-7. doi: 10.1136/sti.70.6.410. PMID: 7705860; PMCID: PMC1195309.

Fernández-Carrasco FJ, Batugg-Chaves C, Ruger-Navarrete A, Riesco-González FJ, Palomo-Gómez R, Gómez-Salgado J, Rodriguez Diaz L, Vázquez-Lara MD, Fagundo-Rivera J, Vázquez-Lara JM. Influence of Pregnancy on Sexual Desire in: Pregnant Women and Their Partners: Systematic Review. Public Health Rev. 2024 Jan 19;44:1606308. doi 10.3389/phrs.2023.1606308. PMID: 38312526; PMCID: PMC10835432.

Garcia MR, Leslie SW, Wray AA. Sexually Transmitted Infections. [Updated 2024 Apr 20]. In: StatPearls [Internet]. Treasure Island (FL) StatPearls Publishing; 2026 Jan-. Available from: https://www.ncbi.nlm.nih.gov/books/NBK560808/

Gold JM, Shrimanker I. Physiology, Vaginal. 2023 Jul 24. In: StatPearls [Internet]. Treasure Island (FL) StatPearls Publishing; 2026 Jan-. PMID: 31424731.

Henigsman, S. A. (2019, April 5) Female sex hormones: Types, roles, and effect on arousal. Www.medicalnewstoday.com. https://www.medicalnewstoday.com/articles/324887#menopause

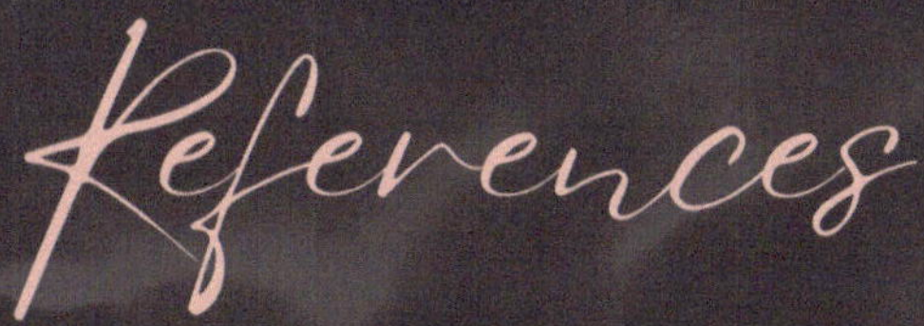

References

Herbenick D, Perry CP, Fortenberry JD, Wasata R, Wilson J, Miller O, Willens K, Williams A, Frey G. Women's Experiences with Exercise-Induced Orgasm: Findings from Qualitative Interviews. Arch Sex Behav. 2025 Oct;54(9):3625-3640. doi: 10.1007/s10508-025-03237-9. Epub 2025 Oct 2. PMID: 41039091; PMCID: PMC12675600.

Hoare BS, Mikes BA, Khan YS. Anatomy, Abdomen and Pelvis: Female Internal Genitals. [Updated 2025 Feb 18]. In: StatPearls [Internet]. Treasure Island (FL): StatPearls Publishing; 2026 Jan-. [Figure, The Female Reproductive System. In females,...] Available from: https://www.ncbi.nlm.nih.gov/books/NBK554601/figure/article-32330.image.f3/

Huang YC, Chang KV. Kegel Exercises. [Updated 2023 May 1]. In: StatPearls [Internet]. Treasure Island (FL): StatPearls Publishing; 2026 Jan-. Available from: https://www.ncbi.nlm.nih.gov/books/NBK555898/?utm_source=chatgpt.com

InformedHealth.org [Internet]. Cologne, Germany: Institute for Quality and Efficiency in Health Care (IQWiG); 2006-. Overview: Heavy periods. [Updated 2025 Feb 25]. Available from: https://www.ncbi.nlm.nih.gov/books/NBK279294/

Kulhawik R, Zborowska K, Grabarek BO, Boroń D, Skrzypulec-Plinta V, Drosdzol-Cop A. Changes in the Sexual Behavior of Partners in Each Trimester of Pregnancy in Otwock in Polish Couples. Int J Environ Res Public Health. 2022 Mar 2;19(5):2921. doi: 10.3390/ijerph19052921. PMID: 35270613; PMCID: PMC8910547.

Kumar P, Magon N. Hormones in pregnancy. Niger Med J. 2012 Oct;53(4):179-83. doi: 10.4103/0300-1652.107549. PMID: 23661874; PMCID: PMC3640235.

Lohova-Matisa E, Rezeberga D, Miskova A. Feminine Intimate Hygiene: A Review of Healthy and Unhealthy Habits in Women. Medicina (Kaunas). 2025 Jul 19;61(7):1302. doi: 10.3390/medicina61071302. PMID: 40731931; PMCID: PMC12300265.

Maharjan, D. T., Syed, A. A. S., Lin, G. N., & Ying, W. (2021). Testosterone in Female Depression: A Meta-Analysis and Mendelian Randomization Study. Biomolecules, 11(3), 409. https://doi.org/10.3390/biom11030409

Maister L, Fotopoulou A, Turnbull O, Tsakiris M. The Erogenous Mirror: Intersubjective and Multisensory Maps of Sexual Arousal in Men and Women. Arch Sex Behav. 2020 Nov;49(8):2919-2933. doi: 10.1007/s10508-020-01756-1. Epub 2020 Jun 12. PMID: 32533518; PMCID: PMC7641941.

Marcin, A., & Santos-Longhurst, A. (2018, January 16). Period Blood Color Chart: Black, Brown, Bright Red, and More. Healthline. https://www.healthline.com/health/womens-health/period-blood#brown

Mikes BA, Wray AA. Gynecologic Pelvic Examination. [Updated 2024 Feb 25]. In: StatPearls [Internet]. Treasure Island (FL): StatPearls Publishing; 2026 Jan-. Available from: https://www.ncbi.nlm.nih.gov/books/NBK534223/

National Academies of Sciences, Engineering, and Medicine; Health and Medicine Division; Board on Population Health and Public Health Practice; Committee on a Framework for the Consideration of Chronic Debilitating Conditions in Women; Batulan Z, Bhimla A, Higginbotham EJ, editors. Advancing Research on Chronic Conditions in Women. Washington (DC): National Academies Press (US); 2024 Sep 25. 5, Female-Specific and Gynecologic Conditions. Available from: https://www.ncbi.nlm.nih.gov/books/NBK607731/

References

National Academies of Sciences, Engineering, and Medicine; Health and Medicine Division; Board on Population Health and Public Health Practice; Committee on a Framework for the Consideration of Chronic Debilitating Conditions in Women; Batulan Z, Bhimla A, Higginbotham EJ, editors. Advancing Research on Chronic Conditions in Women. Washington (DC) National Academies Press (US) 2024 Sep 25. 6, Chronic Conditions That Predominantly Impact or Affect Women Differently. Available from: https://www.ncbi.nlm.nih.gov/books/NBK607719/

National Academies of Sciences, Engineering, and Medicine; Health and Medicine Division; Board on Population Health and Public Health Practice; Committee on the Assessment of NIH Research on Women's Health; Geller A, Salganicoff A, Burke SP, editors. A New Vision for Women's Health Research: Transformative Change at the National Institutes of Health. Washington (DC) National Academies Press (US) 2025 Feb 14. 7, Overview of Selected Women's Health Conditions. Available from: https://www.ncbi.nlm.nih.gov/books/NBK612403/

National Institute of Child Health and Human Development. (2017, January 31) What are some common signs of pregnancy? Https://Www.nichd.nih.gov/. https://www.nichd.nih.gov/health/topics/pregnancy/conditioninfo/signs
Nguyen JD, Fakoya AO, Duong H. Anatomy, Abdomen and Pelvis: Female External Genitalia. [Updated 2025 Feb 15]. In: StatPearls [Internet]. Treasure Island (FL) StatPearls Publishing; 2026 Jan-. Available from: https://www.ncbi.nlm.nih.gov/books/NBK547703/

Oren C, Peled-Avron L, Shamay-Tsoory SG. A scent of romance: human putative pheromone affects men's sexual cognition. Soc Cogn Affect Neurosci. 2019 Jul 31;14(7)719-726. doi: 10.1093/scan/nsz051. PMID: 31309986; PMCID: PMC6778825. Özengin N, Ün Yıldırım N, Duran B. A comparison between stabilization exercises and pelvic floor muscle training in women with pelvic organ prolapse. Turk J Obstet Gynecol. 2015 Mar;12(1)11-17. doi: 10.4274/tjod.74317. Epub 2015 Mar 15. PMID: 28913034; PMCID: PMC5558398.

Pelvic Floor Therapy. (2025, May 29) Hopkinsmedicine.org. https://www.hopkinsmedicine.org/health/treatment-tests-and-therapies/pelvic-floor-therapy?utm_source=chatgpt.com

Ram D, Julakanti P, Atiquzzaman NT, Nagy S, Lin AY, Kesselman MM. Dietary Influence on Bacterial Vaginosis. Cureus. 2025 Sep 29;17(9)e93506. doi: 10.7759/cureus.93506. PMID: 41170228; PMCID: PMC12571456.

Reed BG, Carr BR. The Normal Menstrual Cycle and the Control of Ovulation. [Updated 2018 Aug 5]. In: Feingold KR, Adler RA, Ahmed SF, et al., editors. Endotext [Internet]. South Dartmouth (MA) MDText.com, Inc.; 2000-. Available from: https://www.ncbi.nlm.nih.gov/books/NBK279054/

Scaccia, A. (2020, March 12) How to Masturbate with a Vagina: 28 Tips and Tricks for Solo Play. Healthline; Healthline Media. https://www.healthline.com/health/womens-health/how-to-masturbate-for-women#positions-to-try

Stamos D, Sapouna V, Astraka KM, Thanopoulou S, Giannakis I, Pantou A, Baltogiannis D, Paschopoulos M, Sofikitis N, Zachariou A. Female Sexual Function and Pelvic Floor Muscle Training: A Narrative Review. Cureus. 2025 Jun 11;17(6)e85751. doi: 10.7759/cureus.85751. PMID: 40656351; PMCID: PMC12247012.

References

Stephanie, M. (2023) The Role of Hormones in Women Health. Journal of Women's Health Care, 12(3) 1-2. https://doi.org/10.35248/2167-0420.23.12.633

Sutton, J. (2018, June 5) G Spot in Women: What It Is, How to Find It, and Sex Positions. Healthline. https://www.healthline.com/health/g-spot-in-women

Thiyagarajan DK, Basit H, Jeanmonod R. Physiology, Menstrual Cycle. [Updated 2024 Sep 27]. In: StatPearls [Internet]. Treasure Island (FL) StatPearls Publishing; 2026 Jan-. Available from: https://www.ncbi.nlm.nih.gov/books/NBK500020/

Verhaeghe, J., Gheysen, R., & Enzlin, P. (2013) Pheromones and their effect on women's mood and sexuality. Facts, views & vision in ObGyn, 5(3) 189-195.

Vulvovaginal - STI Treatment Guidelines. (2021, July 14) Cdc.gov. https://www.cdc.gov/std/treatment-guidelines/vaginal-discharge.htm?utm_source=chatgpt.com

Vulvovaginal Health. (2020) Acog.org. https://www.acog.org/womens-health/faqs/vulvovaginal-health?utm_source=chatgpt.com

Walters, M. (2021, September) Is There Really a Connection Between Your Menstrual Cycle and the Moon? Healthline; Healthline Media. https://www.healthline.com/health/womens-health/menstrual-cycle-and-the-moon#takeaway

What Happens at an Ob-Gyn Checkup and Why? One Doctor Explains. (n.d.) Www.acog.org. https://www.acog.org/womens-health/experts-and-stories/the-latest/what-happens-at-an-ob-gyn-checkup-and-why-one-doctor-explains

Wilcox AJ, Dunson D, Baird DD. The timing of the "fertile window" in the menstrual cycle: day specific estimates from a prospective study. BMJ. 2000 Nov 18;321(7271)1259-62. doi: 10.1136/bmj.321.7271.1259. PMID: 11082086; PMCID: PMC27529.

Williams, M. N., & Jacobson, A. (2016) Effect of Copulins on Rating of Female Attractiveness, Mate-Guarding, and Self-Perceived Sexual Desirability. Evolutionary Psychology, 14(2) 1474704916643328. https://doi.org/10.1177/1474704916643328

Wu, Y., Wei, R., Ou, J., Shen, B., & Ye, Y. (2022) Estratetraenol increases preference for large sexual reward but not impulsivity among heterosexual males. Hormones and behavior, 146, 105266. https://doi.org/10.1016/j.yhbeh.2022.105266

Yuhas, D. (2014, May) Human Sexual Responses Boosted by Bodily Scents. Scientific American. https://www.scientificamerican.com/article/human-sexual-responses-boosted-by-bodily-scents/?utm_source=chatgpt.com